HOW TO BUY THE RIGHT HORSE

Carolyn Henderson and Lynn Russell

SWAN·HILL
PRESS

Dedication

To Jack Russell – the only one with two legs – and Jill and Maurice Starbuck,
with thanks for your love and encouragement

Copyright © 1996 Carolyn Henderson
Photographs © John Henderson 1996
First published in the UK in 1996
by Swan Hill Press, an imprint of Airlife Publishing Ltd

British Library Cataloguing in Publication Data
A catalogue record for this book
is available from the British Library

ISBN 1 85310 722 0

Typeset by Hewer Text Composition Services, Edinburgh
Printed in England by The Bath Press, Bath.

Swan Hill Press

an imprint of Airlife Publishing Ltd
101 Longden Road, Shrewsbury SY3 9EB, England

Contents

Chapter 1
The First Considerations

Every week hundreds of horses and ponies are put up for sale through magazine advertisements, at sales and in dealers' yards. Just as many people are searching for their ideal horse, whether it be a top-class competition animal or something to hack out and have fun with. It should be possible to match up buyers and sellers to everyone's satisfaction, but, unfortunately, buying horses is an equation that often adds up to unhappiness.

Buying a horse is never as easy as buying a car, or even a house. There are no rules: you know that if you test drive a Ford Escort the one you buy should behave in the same way, but real horsepower is different. Two horses of the same height, type and age can have totally different characteristics and capabilities, which is where the fascination and frustration of finding the right one starts.

Every time you buy a horse, you have to be prepared that, to a certain extent, you are taking a chance. But by doing your homework you can make sure that the odds are in your favour and the horse you take home will turn out to be the partner you have been hoping for. You owe it to yourself and to your new horse to do everything possible to get it right: he has no say in the matter and that makes your responsibility even tougher.

The perfect horse has yet to be born, although a lot of people find this hard to accept. Just as we are only human, so horses and ponies all have faults or weaknesses. But just as we all like or dislike certain kinds of people, so different horses can be matched up with different owners.

In the same way, horses vary in their natural aptitudes and talents. With the right schooling, the right care and the right rider, any horse should be able to go nicely on the flat, jump adequately and be pleasant to own and look after. But as you might have a natural artistic or literary gift but be clumsy at anything demanding practical skills, so horses vary in their abilities.

A Thoroughbred horse with the speed, stamina and scope to make an eventer might well be unsuitable for pure dressage at a high level. Similarly, an Arab who effortlessly eats up the miles in endurance riding could be a square peg in a round hole if his rider wants to concentrate on show jumping. It sounds and is obvious, yet a lot of riders think 'I like the look of this horse, therefore it will have to do what I want it to' or even worse, 'This horse is cheap, therefore it must be the right one.'

Working out the right match is a mixture of honesty and skill, with a bit of luck thrown in. You must provide the honesty, this book shares the necessary skills and the luck is an unknown quantity! There is an old saying that in buying horses, you never know what you've got until you've got it home: as with many horsey homilies, it contains a lot of truth.

Good horse dealers say that an honest buyer and an honest seller will always strike a deal. There is more to that simple statement than at first meets the eye: most prospective buyers and sellers would be very offended if they were accused of being dishonest, but it is often true even when they have the best intentions. Sometimes there may be a fine line between the person who is dishonest and the one who is unrealistic or even lacks knowledge, but the results can be just as unhappy.

When you are looking for a horse, you must be absolutely honest with yourself about what you want to do, how capable you are as a rider and how much money you have to spend. Horse buyers can be divided into three categories: 20 per cent know exactly what they want, 70 per cent have a reasonable idea and 10 per cent do not have a clue and often end up with an animal that is totally unsuitable.

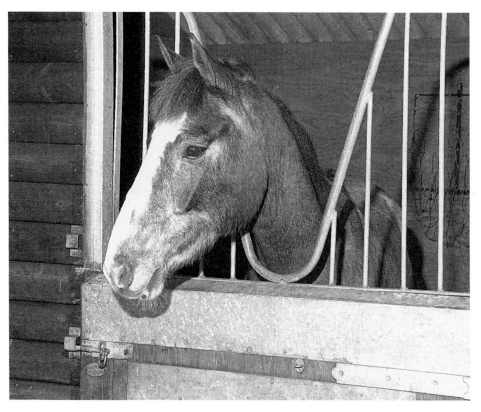

Buying the horse you will want to see every day is a big decision.

It can be a good idea, especially if you are buying your first horse or do not really know what sort you should be looking for, to sit down with a piece of paper and write down what sort of riding or competition programme you would like to follow. Do you want to have a go at most riding club activities—a bit of dressage, a bit of show jumping and a bit of cross-country? Does the idea of showing appeal? Or do you fancy aiming at endurance riding? Then again, maybe you want a horse or pony that everyone in the family can ride, and perhaps drive as well.

You may have to accept that the sort of horse that will make an ideal partner now may not always be able to fill that role. You may be lucky: there are cases when horses bought just for fun have turned out to be real stars in top level competition, but they are the exception rather than the rule. But no matter how lofty your dreams, remember that they lie in the future: you have to deal with the here and now.

There is nothing wrong with longing to ride round Badminton or parade under the Wembley spotlights. But even if you can afford to buy a horse with this sort of talent, the purchase could be disastrous. If you do not have the ability to make use of his, you will both suffer in the long run. It is far better to say to yourself that whilst one day you hope to ride at Badminton, the first stepping stone must be a reliable horse with the experience to take you safely round novice events. If he turns out to have the ability to progress, all well and good but if not, you may have to sell him to a suitable home and then move on to another, more talented horse. Pushing a horse to do more than he is capable of only leads to unhappiness on both sides.

When you are buying a horse, especially if it is your first one, you obviously do not want to think about selling him. Unfortunately, you have to: you may be lucky enough to find a horse that you never want or have to part with, but life does not always work out like that. Circumstances and priorities change, so always think about today first and tomorrow later.

A bold rider needs a bold horse.

Once you have worked out your priorities, it is time to take a long and perhaps slightly painful look at your own capabilities. It is often said that looking after and riding horses is character building, but it is also good for character analysis! Start with the basics: your height, weight, and whether or not you are physically strong. Then turn to something equally important but often forgotten—your temperament.

Everyone knows that a horse's temperament must be taken into consideration, but a lot of people do not realise that their own matters just as much. There is an old saying that opposites attract, but this does not always work with horses. Sometimes you can make a better relationship with an animal whose characteristics are similar to your own.

This is where honesty comes in, because you must decide whether you have a strong or a weak personality. Neither has to be necessarily good or bad: a strong character does not have to be aggressive, and in the same way a weaker one is not automatically a wimp. Only you know if you are the sort of person who will go all out for something important, or if you are the anything for a quiet life type.

Your horse's personality should match your own as far as possible. A dominant horse needs a dominant rider, though this does not mean someone who bullies or forces him. You can be sympathetic as well as strong. But give this horse to a weak, perhaps hesitant owner and you have a recipe for disaster. The horse will run rings round the rider and you could end up in an unpleasant and even dangerous situation.

A dominant rider on a weaker horse is not so bad, as sometimes a confident rider can give courage to a hesitant horse. Even so, the time may come when the rider does not have enough bottle for both of them, and when this happens you can come unstuck in a big way. Gutsy, bold riders are far better off on mounts of similar character.

You and the horse also need to be similar in build. There is a crude but effective adage: look at the rider's backside and pick a horse with one to match! In other words, a short, generously built lady would look perfectly at home on a cob but out of place on a lightweight show hack. You may often see exceptions to this guideline in the show ring, but remember that a lot of top show riders are professionals who are used to riding animals of all shapes, sizes and temperaments. They are usually excellent riders who school their horses to perfection, and that eight stone woman on a heavyweight cob or hunter will have done an awful lot of work on the horse at home to produce her faultless display in the ring.

Many people overhorse themselves, and it is usually for one of three reasons—all of which are wrong. The first is that they think only a 16.2hh horse is capable of competing successfully; the second is that they do not realise that a horse's conformation is more important than its size; and the third is simply that they think they look good on a big horse—but if it is not suitable for them this is a bit like buying a Porsche when you lack the driving skills to make the most of it. In other words, they want to pose!

A tall, well-built, long-legged rider obviously needs a big horse. But as a general rule, someone of about five foot four to five foot six is best suited by a well-made 15.2–16hh horse. If you are about five foot two you will probably be happiest with a 15–15.2hh and if you are about four foot ten to five foot a 14–14.2hh should be ideal. Even these guidelines are open to interpretation: for instance, many 14.2hh native ponies will have enough depth of girth to be large enough for a small adult, and in fact their riders may look better on them than on a taller but narrower Thoroughbred who is shallower through the girth.

There is no point in over-horsing yourself.

Competing may demand that you work to a different criteria but even then, it is a mistake to over-horse yourself. Plenty of horses under 16hh have done well at top level: Mark Todd's Charisma was only 15.3hh, but he had the courage and ability to win everything, including Olympic gold medals. A competent rider, even someone small and lightweight, should be happy on anything up to 16.2hh, but once you go over that you need to be very careful.

The really big horses are, unfortunately, often harder to keep sound. This is simply due to their feet and limbs having to support a far greater body-weight. Because of this, they can be more prone to leg injuries and concussion problems, which are the commonest causes of unsoundness. Very big horses are usually long striding and this can make them less handy; a 16hh horse might find a fifth leg to help you out of trouble, but a 17.2hh is more likely to bury you!

The biggest problem with height is that many people do not measure their horses correctly. Sometimes they do not measure them at all, but guess and advertise their 15.2hh as standing 16hh. A well-proportioned, up to height 15.2–16hh horse is plenty big enough for most people; correct proportions are more important than height.

It can be interesting to stand at the ringside at a big show and watch showing classes that have height restrictions on them. People will often say that show horses are over height, when in fact they are well-made. A good small hunter that is a full 15.2hh can be a lot of horse and a show cob, which must not exceed 15.1hh, will carry anyone! You also have to remember that a good show horse will have presence, that 'Look at me' quality which always makes it look bigger than it is.

Matching horse to rider is obviously more difficult when the animal is to be ridden by two or even more people. The commonest situation is when a husband and wife want a horse they can both enjoy riding, perhaps one to compete and the other to hack or hunt. They should be quite easy to suit if they are of similar height and build, but a lot of careful thought is required if there is a big difference between them. The breeder who produces the first adjustable horse will make a lot of money. Until then, the answer is compromise with the scales being tipped in the direction of whoever will use the horse most.

Let us take a typical example: a six-foot, thirteen stone man and his five-foot-five, nine stone wife. He wants to hack once or twice a week and do the occasional sponsored ride and small show, and she wants to compete at top-class riding club level. As she will do most of the riding, we need to look for a horse that suits her but which is comfortable for her husband to ride and can take his weight happily.

A horse or pony should be the right height and type for his rider.

The type of horse that would suit this combination would be a 16hh middleweight that has good conformation and is deep through the girth, or a well-mannered, compact animal that is an inch or two bigger or a quality cob which moves or jumps well. The ones to avoid are the tall, leggy Thoroughbreds who are not deep enough to take the husband's length of leg and probably would not have enough bone to be up to his weight or the horse who has a substantial body on spindly legs.

Other considerations that need to be dealt with before you even look at a horse are your ability, the amount of money you have to spend and the facilities and help that are available to you once you have obtained your new purchase. If you are inexperienced it is a good idea to buy a horse that already has some decent all-round experience. If you want to specialise, then by all means concentrate on ability for the discipline that attracts you but, as we have already warned, keep your ambitions at a reasonable level. It is a waste of time and money as well as being unfair to the horse to buy a top-class dressage star when you want to start at local level.

For most people, a horse has to fit in with the demands of work and home. This may mean there are times when you cannot ride, possibly for several days at a time. In the depths of winter, perhaps you will only be able to ride at weekends. Unless you intend to keep your horse at full livery or have someone reliable to exercise him during the week, your horse will need to be turned out every day. Can you provide shelter, rugs and adequate feed to keep him in good condition? If you want to buy a Thoroughbred or a horse with a high percentage of Thoroughbred blood, can you afford the running costs? He will need a lot more hard food and rugs than a half-bred horse or a cob.

Money is one of the most basic considerations of all. Most of us have to put a limit on the purchase price of a horse, whether it is £2,000, £3,000 or £10,000. So before you start making inquiries try looking through some of the adverts and work out whether you can afford the sort of horse you would like, or will have to compromise in some way.

There is no point in ringing up about a £4,000 horse if you only have £2,500 to spend. Some sellers might be prepared to haggle a bit, but you have to be realistic. If you are not, you are guilty of becoming the worst kind of person in the whole business of buying and selling horses—a time waster.

If scanning the adverts shows that you cannot afford your dream horse, you have two options: one is to wait until your savings have increased, and the other is to look at animals that are older or younger than the prime time five to eight age group.

An older horse of, say, ten or twelve that has good conformation (see Chapter 2) will be cheaper and should have a good working life left to him. The disadvantage is that if you want to sell him in a couple of years and buy something to match your increased ambitions and ability, it might be harder to find him a new home.

Riders who are reasonably experienced and have a good teacher to help them might enjoy bringing on a young horse. A green four-year-old might be cheaper than a made horse, though occasionally some people ask a lot for unproven potential and others are prepared to pay for it. Remember that it takes an expert to spot real potential, and even then there are a lot of ugly ducklings that never turn into swans.

Sadly, there is no such thing as a January sale in the horse world. Bargains are few and far between, and unlikely to fall into the hands of the amateur. A cheap horse usually has a problem and should only be bought by the professional or semiprofessional who has the knowledge and time to sort it out.

Admittedly we have already acknowledged that the perfect horse does not exist, and throughout this book we will look at what may or may not be acceptable. But as far as the ordinary horse owner goes, there are some things that should never be compromised on: they may be for reasons of safety, or simply because having a horse ought to be a pleasure, not a series of problems. If you fall into that category, then avoid any horse that is unreliable in traffic, naps, rears, refuses to be caught or to load or has stable vices that affect its condition.

Most people need a horse who is good in traffic.

The roads are so busy now that a horse that is frightened of or naughty in traffic is a liability to all. It just is not worth the risk, even if you think you will only ride on bridleways; the time will come when you have to take the animal on the roads, and you will not only be risking your life but also the lives of other road users. You also have to remember that the horse will be difficult to sell if you ever need to part with him.

Napping and rearing are problems for the professional to sort out, and a horse that is bad to catch or load is, quite frankly, a pain. There is nothing worse than coming home from work and not being able to ride because dear little Dobbin refuses to be caught, or spending hours on a showground trying to persuade him to go back in the horsebox or trailer.

Stable vices, which are looked at in more depth later on, are another problem. Crib biting and windsucking affect a horse's digestion and therefore its condition; many people think weaving is more acceptable, though it depends on its degree of severity.

If you are worried about going it alone, you can always ask a friendly expert for advice, but please make sure that your expert is just that. Choose a real horseman or woman, someone with his or her own yard who is or has been successful—not a friend who thinks she knows a bit or a newly qualified eighteen-year-old BHSAI who knows the answers to all the exam questions but does not yet have the necessary practical experience.

Hopefully the seller will be as honest as you are, but this does not always follow. Some dishonesty is down to ignorance and the rest is an understandable desire to represent their animal in the best possible light. Flick through any issue of a magazine such as *Horse and Hound* and you will see pages of advertisements for paragons on four legs: potential three-day eventers, show horses that are bound to get to Wembley and hunters that will jump everything, all day long.

As soon as you start looking at these equine superstars in the flesh you will realise that the reality does not always match the advert: sometimes it will not look anything like it. Later on we will consider how to translate the adverts and avoid wasting both your time and that of the vendor, but be prepared from the start to find plenty of swine amongst the pearls.

By now you are probably thinking that buying a horse is not such a good idea after all and that showing goldfish might be less stressful. It is certainly not something that should be undertaken lightly. There are so many things to take into consideration before you even start that it is not until we get to Chapter 4 that we even think about reading the For Sale adverts! But as you read through this book you will discover that looking for your ideal horse is not that bad: it can even be fun, and hopefully you will be able to find the one that is as near perfect for you as possible.

Chapter 2
Conformation

Whatever job your new horse is intended to do, whether it be hacking or three-day eventing, you want him to stay sound and athletic. This means he must have the right make and shape. Good conformation is a blueprint for efficiency and affects everything from whether a horse is a comfortable ride to how easy (or difficult) he finds it to work on the bit or jump.

A lot of people say that it does not matter what a horse looks like as long as he can do what you want him to. To a certain extent, that is true. But whilst you have to be realistic and prepared to compromise, you must always have an ideal in your mind as this is your yardstick. The good news is that it is fairly easy to define what perfect conformation should be; the bad news is that you will never find it! The perfect horse has yet to be born, for the simple reason that horses are not machines.

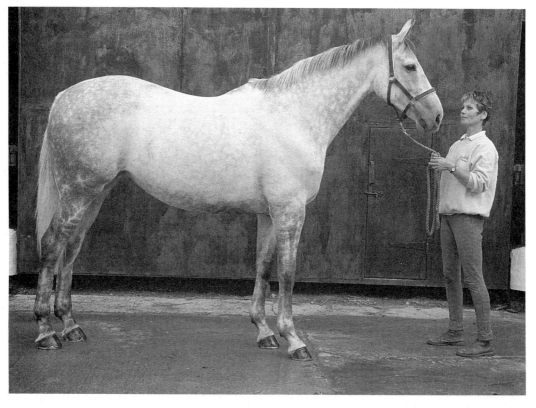

A substantial Thoroughbred with excellent conformation.

Judging conformation, or getting an eye for a horse, is not a mysterious gift that some people are born with and others can never master. It is an acquired skill that comes through practice and experience. A lot of people ride horses without really looking at them, but if you compare what you see in front of you to the feel you get when you ride the horse, you will learn what is important and how to weigh good points against bad.

The real skill comes in deciding what you can live with and what makes you decide to reject a horse. Different riders have different priorities, and particular likes and dislikes are tempered by past experiences. For instance, if you owned a horse with very upright pasterns that developed ringbone, you would probably be less likely to forgive that particular conformation defect in future purchases.

You need to learn how to look at a horse both as a whole and as a collection of individual components. One fault in isolation is rarely enough to make you rule out a horse, unless it is exaggerated, but two or more together may add up to such a combination of weakness or vulnerability that you do not want to take a chance. For instance, a hind leg that is slightly straight may not be too bad on its own, but couple it with a long back and weak quarters and this can often give trouble.

You can always ask other people's advice on conformation, but in the end the buck stops with you. If you really like a horse, so much so that you want to give him the benefit of the doubt, then have him vetted. If the vet says he is suitable, then take a chance. But if your doubts exceed your optimism, this is not the one for you. There is always another day and another horse.

The final thing to remember before you assess a horse is that the most important part of his conformation is the bit between the ears. If the horse does not have a good mind, you are buying heartbreak. Even if he scores ten out of ten on every conformation test, a suspect temperament will always let him down when the pressure is on.

Nasty or unstable horses are, fortunately, very rare. Aggressive horses have often been made that way by incorrect handling and most, some people would say all, behavioural problems have the same root cause. However, horses vary in their temperaments as much as people: some are placid, others sharp and quick to react. The sort of person who likes sensitive horses is often driven to distraction by the anything for a quiet life type, and vice versa.

Professional riders can get the best out of any horse, and usually have a more businesslike attitude to their animals; most owners have to like a horse to live with it, though. And whilst it may be possible to cure behavioural problems or minimise them to an acceptable level, you will not change a horse's personality. A sensitive horse may become more relaxed, but he will never turn into a laid-back patent safety.

Finally, you cannot ignore the illogical and sometimes annoying gut reaction that makes you like or dislike a horse. If the horse has good conformation, a willing temperament and does everything asked of him to the best of his ability, the chances are that you will be quite happy to live with him. Unfortunately, there are sometimes inexplicable and illogical occasions when you meet a horse who on paper could be what you are looking for but, in practice, you know that he is not the one.

Your head should rule your heart for 99 per cent of the time when you are buying a horse. However, there is still that little bit of leeway for acting on what your heart tells you. You are the one who is going to have to look at him and after him day after day, and there will be times when only the fact that you like him enables you to do it cheerfully. If you start off thinking 'You're a really nice horse, but I don't really want to see your head over my door every day,' then he is not the one for you.

Overall impressions

People often say that they looked at a horse's head over the stable door and decided to buy him there and then. This means they either like living dangerously or have more than their fair share of luck! You may base your first impression of a horse from the shape of his head, but try not to be swayed too much by it.

Instead, look at the horse as a whole without focusing on any particular part. It may be that something is so glaringly bad that your eye is drawn straight to it, but more often than not the horse will present a generally balanced or unbalanced picture. Does he look all in one piece or does the front end somehow not match the back one? Does his shape flow from one part to the other, or is your eye caught by a series of disjointed angles? Do his limbs match his body or does he look as if he has borrowed them from another horse, usually because they are too fine and spindly for a chunky body?

Your sense of proportion will tell you a lot, but there are more accurate guides to help you. As a start, stand the horse so that he is balanced and draw an imaginary square round his body, as shown in the diagram. Ideally, he should fill a perfect square. If you look at him from behind, you should be able to draw a square round his hindquarters and one the same size from the ground to the points of his hocks.

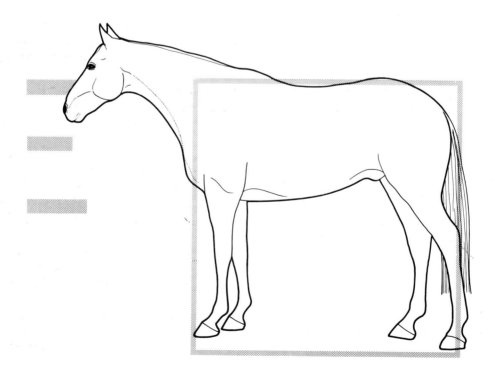

Another way of assessing his proportions is to compare a series of measurements. This is often easier to do on a photograph and can be an interesting exercise to get your eye in. The length of head, measurement of shoulder, depth of body, length from stifle to hock and from hock to ground should all be about the same. In the same way, the length of neck should be the same as a measurement taken from the highest point of the withers to the croup.

As you look at a horse, gauge whether his musculature is symmetrical. A young horse will lack muscle on his neck, topline and quarters, whereas an older horse who has been worked correctly will have developed the muscles in these areas. Warning bells should ring if the muscle development seems lopsided—for instance, if his quarters look rounded on one side when you stand behind him but slope sharply away on the other. This is often a sign of a previous injury.

Once you have formed an overall mental picture of the horse, you can study his individual parts. There are different ways of doing this: some people start at the ground and work their way up, their reasoning being that the feet and legs are the most important factors in keeping a horse sound; others start at the front and work their way back, which helps to give an idea of whether the horse has a flowing or disjointed shape.

Head, neck and shoulders

Let us start with the head over the stable door. It does not matter whether it is pretty or plain, unless you are buying a show horse of a particular type and even then, the right sort of bridle can make a marked difference. It is important that the horse has a kind outlook; laid back ears and snapping teeth do not make for a good beginning.

The head and neck are the horse's balancing rod and so should look as if they belong together. A horse with a big head will be better balanced if his neck is on the short side. A big head on a long neck puts so much weight on the forehand that the horse will feel as if he is going downhill when being ridden. Similarly, a small head gives better overall balance if it is set on a longish neck.

Although it is nice to see a large eye, do not automatically discount a horse with smaller ones. They are not always the sign of an ungenerous temperament—piggy eyes do not necessarily mean piggy horses! Similarly, a white ring all the way round a horse's eyes does not necessarily indicate an uncertain temperament. Some horses have a bump between their eyes, and many horse people swear it is a sign of an uncertain or stubborn temperament. Again, bear this in mind but treat every horse as an individual.

Look in the horse's mouth, not only to get an idea of his age but also to see if he is likely to suffer any eating problems. The upper and lower incisors should have an even bite and the horse should not be badly overshot or undershot. An overshot mouth, where the upper jaw is too long, is often called a parrot mouth; both this and an undershot jaw, where the top jaw is too short, can make it difficult for the horse to chew his food properly. The knock-on effects can be a tendency to colic, because the horse does not digest his food efficiently, or difficulty in keeping weight on for the same reason.

The angle where the head joins the neck should not be too sharp, or the horse will find it difficult to flex and may make a noise in his breathing when asked to do so. The way the neck is set on to the withers is also important: if the neck is set on low, the horse will be harder to train than one who is naturally born on the bit.

The worst type of neck conformation is the ewe neck, which looks as if it is set on upside down. Horses made this way often have little muscle development on top of their necks and too much underneath it, usually because they have been forced into an outline they are not built to work in and have fought against it. It often takes a skilled eye to tell whether a ewe neck has been caused by bad riding or is a genuine conformational fault; correct schooling can remedy the first but not the second.

A swan neck, which is unnaturally high and arched, is the opposite side of the coin. It may even look attractive to an uneducated eye, but this sort of horse often goes behind the bit and will tuck his nose in rather than work through and round from behind. A horse's engine is in his hind legs and the power must come from there if he is to be truly on the bit.

Withers only cause problems if they are too high or non-existent, both of which can make fitting a saddle difficult. If the horse has a good shoulder then a poorly defined wither is not necessarily a drawback; problems arise from straight shoulders with no withers, so the saddle inevitably slides forwards. High withers make it more difficult to balance a saddle so that it sits correctly and gives sufficient clearance.

The shape of a horse's shoulder has a marked effect on his movement and the sort of ride he gives. A straight shoulder, which is often coupled with upright pasterns, gives an up and down action that is fine for a driving horse but uncomfortable in a riding one. It also causes saddle fitting problems because the saddle often slips forwards and digs in to the muscles behind the withers. A sloping shoulder makes for a more comfortable ride and often helps the horse's jumping ability—he finds it easier to lift his forearm over a fence.

Judging the shape of a shoulder, as with so many conformation points, is easier if the horse is in slightly lean condition. An experienced eye will not be deceived by excess weight, but an inexperienced one often is.

Feet and limbs

If a horse does not have good legs and feet, forget it. The old saying, 'No foot, no horse' is as true today as it ever was: a good farrier can do a lot to help the less than perfect, but it still pays to be choosy. Never underestimate the stress that the limbs and feet are asked to take: they may have to support 600kg of body-weight, and when a horse lands over a fence, there is a short period when one limb has to support a force equivalent to many times that.

First check that the horse has two matching pairs of feet. Hind feet are usually slightly smaller than forefeet, but each pair should be the same size and shape. A lot of people find it difficult to judge foot conformation because they cannot tell the difference between bad feet and bad shoeing, but if one foot is bigger than the other or the angles are noticeably different, be careful. If you really like the horse, see what your vet says when he carries out the pre-purchase examination.

The size of the feet will obviously vary in relation to the size of the horse, but they should be in proportion. You do not want to see a cob with pony feet or a Thoroughbred with soup plates. Narrow, boxy feet seem to be predisposed to concussion problems, especially if the horse also has upright pasterns.

When you pick up the feet, the frogs should be well defined and the heels not too low or weak; the latter is often a problem in Thoroughbred horses, but can sometimes be improved by good shoeing. For some reason many racing people have their horses' feet shaped so they are longer in the toe than is normally ideal, which puts extra weight on the heels.

Look at the soles of the feet, too. If they are flat, which is common conformation in a lot of Irish Draught crosses, the horse will be more prone to bruising than the horse with slightly concave soles. Again, a good farrier can do a lot to help.

The angle at which the foot joins the limb is important. There should be a continuous slope from the pastern down the hoof wall; if the angle is broken, the horse will be susceptible to concussion. Check that the coronet is free from lumps or ridges, which could be a sign of ringbone (an arthritic condition.)

It is always nice to find a horse with clean limbs (in other words, with no lumps or bumps) but you have to accept that if he has done a fair amount of work, there may be minor signs of wear and tear. Most people can live with these, as long as they are not going to cause further problems, but be careful about a young horse who shows marked signs of wear. Either he has been pushed too hard, too soon or there are weak links in his conformation that may eventually lead to unsoundness.

The forearm should be broad and long, running into a wide, flat knee and short cannon bones. This conformation gives a good stride and enables the horse to stand up to work. If the horse has a concave outline between the bottom of the knee and the top of the fetlock, he is back at the knee; if the outline is convex, he is over at the knee. Both are faults that can put extra strain on the tendons, but are usually only a problem if they appear in any marked degree. Some horses are tied at the knee, which means there is a noticeable indentation at the back of it; again, it usually only affects the horse if it is particularly noticeable.

When you look at the horse from the front, the cannon bone should come straight down from the centre of the knee. If it is offset, the limb has to take extra strain. Similarly, a horse whose feet turn in or out may be predisposed to concussion problems because one part of the foot takes more concussion than it should.

Splints—bony growths on the splint or cannon bones caused by strain or blows—are the most common foreleg defects. They can also be found on the hind legs, although these are not as common. Splints rarely cause soundness problems once they are formed, unless they are in a position where they interfere with the knee joint.

A horse needs to be able to carry not only his rider's weight but also his own. One of the factors that decides how much weight a horse can carry is the quality and quantity of his bone. This is a measurement taken round the widest part of the cannon bone, just below the knee. Build and bone should be comparable; a small, lightweight Thoroughbred may only have seven inches of bone whereas a cob or heavyweight hunter should measure at least nine and a half inches. What you do not want to see is the horse with a substantial body and spindly legs.

Although the amount of bone is important, it is not the whole story. Flat bone is a better weight bearer than round bone; when you put your hand round the horse's leg, you will be able to feel the difference. Arabs and Thoroughbreds have denser bone than cold-blooded types and if its overall conformation is good, then such a horse with, say, eight inches of bone may be up to more weight than you would think.

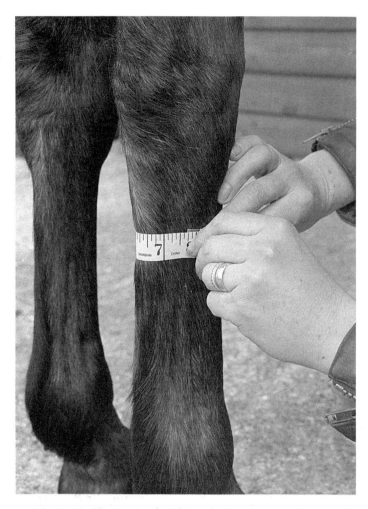

The amount of bone helps to determine a horse's weight carrying ability.

The fetlocks should look as if they are a pair, a rule that applies to all joints. Be careful about lumps on the fetlock, which could be a sign of an arthritic problem, but do not be too concerned about windgalls in a mature horse. These are enlargements of fluid sacs around the pasterns or fetlock joints and can be found either in front or behind.

The pasterns should be reasonably long and sloping if the horse is to be a comfortable ride. If a horse has the right slope to his shoulder, he usually has the right slope to his pasterns; likewise, a horse who is straight in the shoulder often, but not always, is upright in his pasterns.

The hind legs are just as important as the forelegs—in fact, they are probably even more so, because this is where the horse's engine is sited. The second thigh should be reasonably long if the horse is to be an athletic mover and jumper, but do not worry if it seems to lack muscle in a young or unschooled horse. It will soon develop with correct work and feeding.

Hock joints do a lot of hard work and a poorly made hind leg will soon show the strain. A good hock joint should be wide, deep and not too straight. The weakest kind of hock is the sickle hock, where the leg is in front of an imaginary perpendicular line dropped from the point of the hock to the ground. In really bad cases, the horse looks as if he is about to sit down. Cow hocks, which turn inwards, are not usually such a problem unless the fault is very pronounced.

In some horses the natural depression in front of the hock looks as if it is filled in. This is a bog spavin, which is unsightly but technically not an unsoundness unless there are changes in the bone (which would only show up on X-ray.) Bone spavins, which do not show up to the naked eye, are more serious. The first hint that one might be a problem is often that the horse goes lame on a hind leg flexion test.

Curbs, which are swellings on the back of the hind leg just below the hock, can also be a sign of weakness but only if they are true curbs. To find out, pick up the horse's hind leg: if the swelling disappears, it is a false curb and nothing to worry about. If it remains, it is a true curb and something to be discussed with your vet.

Thoroughpins—swellings just above the hock joint and just below the Achilles tendon—are blemishes, but will not usually make a horse lame. Capped hocks, where the points of the hocks fill with fluid and become enlarged, are also unsightly but not an unsoundness. They are usually caused by the horse digging holes in his bedding and scraping his hocks on the bare patches of floor when he gets up.

Body, back and quarters

For the horse to function as an athlete, the sum of his parts must equal a harmonious whole. So whilst the shape of his body may seem less important than a set of good limbs and feet, it is still important. For instance, a horse who is built downhill, with his croup higher than his withers, will always be naturally on his forehand and it will take a lot of schooling to teach him to carry himself in balance.

Starting at the front, does the horse have a reasonably broad chest or does he look as if both legs come out of the same hole? These horses are often poor movers, simply because their legs are so close together they cannot avoid knocking one against the other. On the other hand, a horse who is overly broad in the chest often has a rolling gait that makes him uncomfortable to ride.

The horse who is deep through the girth has plenty of room for his heart and lungs, which adds to his athletic ability. He is also easier to keep condition on than the shallow girthed or herring-gutted animal that always looks run up, rather like a greyhound. The saddle on such a horse is often inclined to slip back, though a good saddle fitter should be able to help solve the problem.

The horse's back may seem a convenient place to put a saddle, but unfortunately for us and even more unfortunately for him he was not actually designed to carry a rider. A reasonably but not over exaggeratedly short back is the strongest kind; horses which are long in the back are often comfortable rides, but length is also a sign of weakness. Mares are usually slightly longer in the back than geldings, to allow enough room to carry a foal.

When you look at the horse from the side, his back should appear just about level; there is a curve to the back, but it is so gentle as to be barely noticeable. A dipped or sway back is a sign of weakness; horses' backs often dip as they get older and their muscles lose the elasticity of youth. Needless to say, the same laws of gravity apply to people: we all tend to sag a bit as we get older! A roach back, which curves upwards, is usually fairly strong. Its drawback is that it makes saddle fitting difficult and the horse is often not particularly comfortable.

This powerful four-year-old is still growing and is higher behind than in front. He is not a show horse, but is sound, tough and a talented jumper.

Growing youngsters always go through a phase when the croup is higher than the withers. Usually things even themselves up, though it may not stop you biting your nails and wondering if your ugly duckling is going to turn into a swan or simply become an ugly duck. However, the horse who stays markedly croup high will always be inclined to go on his forehand and may feel as if the back end is always trying to overtake the front. This type of horse will always need very careful saddle fitting, as the saddle will be inclined to slip forwards and dig into the muscles behind the withers. On the plus side, a lot of good jumpers seem to be slightly croup high and/or to have a pronounced croup known colloquially as a jumper's bump.

Although hindquarters that are naturally weak will always stay that way, muscle development can only be built up through work. Do not confuse muscle with fat: the overweight horse with the backside that looks like an apple from behind is not necessarily muscled up.

With horses, it is all too easy to become obsessive. If you like a horse's temperament and enjoy the ride he gives you, accept that he is bound to have conformation minuses as well as pluses. It is all too easy to read books like this and reject every horse you look at, which does not help anyone—least of all you! Keep your mind as open as your eyes when you look at a horse, and remember that a good horse vet can help you make a common sense judgement.

Remember, too, that you are the one who has to live with the horse. If there is something about him that you really do not like, even if it is his colour, then he is not the one for you. Horses cost enough money and cause enough problems without you finding something to dislike every time you see them!

Movement

Movement and conformation are usually tied together, though occasionally you get a surprise: a good looking horse who disappoints as soon as he is not standing still, or a common type who displays breathtaking paces. Good movement comes from the shoulder, not the elbow; the horse who does not use his shoulder will never be a free, athletic mover even if he moves perfectly straight. Straight movement is lovely to see and is an essential for the show horse, but slight deviations are not usually a reason to turn down an otherwise nice performance horse.

The most common defects in movement are brushing and dishing. Brushing, where the horse knocks one leg against the other, may be caused by conformation, weakness or both. If the legs are too close together, a horse will often not be able to avoid knocking himself and you will have to decide whether wearing protective boots will give him enough protection. Young horses with good basic conformation sometimes brush or knock themselves simply because they are gangly and unbalanced, and the problem disappears as they become stronger and better balanced.

Dishing, where the horse throws one or both front legs out to the side, is only a problem if the fault is exaggerated. True dishing, where the leg is thrown out from the shoulder, is much worse than turning a toe, when the faulty movement starts from lower down the leg. There is an old Irish saying that a horse who dishes will never fall over!

Plaiting, where the horse crosses his front legs as he moves, is not seen very often but, when it is, can be most disconcerting to the onlooker! Surprisingly, horses that move like this do not trip themselves up and fall over as often as you might imagine. As with all deviations from the straight and true, it puts unwanted strain on the limbs.

Chapter 3
Horses for Courses

The blueprint for ideal conformation stays the same whether you are looking for a show hunter or an event horse, and two priorities always stay at the top of the list: the horse must have a temperament you can live with, and any conformation defects must not be so great that they prejudice his soundness. After that, it is a matter of horses for courses: what is vital to a dressage rider may not be so important to an endurance riding specialist.

The dressage horse should be athletic, rhythmic and amenable to training.

This chapter is meant to offer food for thought if you want to buy a horse to do a particular job. It is not meant to imply that there are rules written in stone, such as a top level event horse must be a Thoroughbred, or that only an Arab will succeed in endurance riding. You only have to look at what is happening in the competition world to realise that as soon as rules are written, someone can give you an exception to them. For instance, there are native ponies doing well in all spheres, including an Exmoor pony who is an endurance specialist and a Fell pony who is consistent in Medium level dressage. One of the top endurance horses in Britain is an Anglo-Arab cross Trakehner mare.

Dressage

The dressage horse should present a picture of athleticism and harmony. As soon as he enters the arena, the judge should start thinking positively about how he is going to mark the partnership. Judges are only human and first impressions do matter.

Any well schooled horse or pony can perform a Preliminary or Novice dressage test well, but if you want to progress to and win at higher levels, you need an attractive, free moving horse who finds it easy to work in a collected outline. He should have presence— that look at me quality also so essential in the show horse—but not boil over when put under pressure. In other words, we are back to that magic word: temperament.

Horse and rider should suit each other. Nothing looks more incongruous than a small rider perched on top of an enormous, old-fashioned type of warmblood (see Chapter 4). Fortunately, lightness and grace have regained their importance in modern dressage and lighter types of warmblood and horses with predominantly Thoroughbred blood are gaining high marks.

If you get a pure Thoroughbred who enjoys his flatwork, you can have a very good horse for this discipline. Inevitably, some are square pegs in round holes; in particular, horses bred for Flat racing are bred and build for speed, with low set on necks and a tendency to be croup high, which makes it difficult for them to cope with advanced work such as Piaffe.

You will have a head start if you buy a horse who has a good shoulder and a well set on head and neck, so that he is born on the bit and built to give you a good ride. Surprisingly, perfect movement is not at the top of many international riders' lists of priority: they believe that if a horse moves freely from the shoulder and has a natural rhythm to his stride, it does not matter if he does not move perfectly straight. Watch a lot of top horses coming up the centre line and you will see that more than a few have a slight dish! Obviously it is lovely to have a horse with three fantastic paces, but if you have to compromise, most trainers believe that the walk is the hardest pace to improve and the trot the easiest. A good walk usually means a good canter; racehorse trainers predict yearlings' ability to gallop on the quality of their walk.

Some riders believe that slight sickle hocks, which are a weakness, can enhance the impression that the horse is putting its back legs underneath itself and working through from behind. Quite honestly, any judge who is fooled by this should not be judging at all. Similarly, the idea that one white sock gives the impression that the horse moves unevenly might be a useful excuse, but is probably no more than that.

The way a horse goes is, of course, largely down to the way he is trained and ridden. But if he has plenty of room between the jawbones and the angle of throat and neck is not too sharp, he will find it much easier to flex.

Vets say that *sacro iliac* injuries are quite common in dressage horses, but how many are due to conformation and how many can be laid at the door of poor riding and management is a matter for debate. Even if you have a horse with particularly good conformation through his back, loins and quarters, you still need to pay careful attention to warming up before work and cooling down afterwards.

Show jumping

As the horse world has become more scientific and detailed research has gone into feeding and management, it seems strange that there have been hardly any scientific studies into conformation. The major exception is a study carried out in the 1970s into the characteristics of talented jumpers.

A youngster that shows this sort of technique over a pole should have promise as a show jumper. This is the horse on page 24 in the winter of his third year - you need to be able to see beyond a woolly coat and immature frame!

The most significant finding was that horses with natural jumping ability were longer than average from stifle to hock. They also had longer than average forearms, which enabled them to pick up in front. The length of the cannon bones did not appear to have any relation to the horse's ability, though as shorter cannon bones indicate greater strength, they would still be an advantage from the point of view of soundness.

The research showed that a longer neck was an advantage for a jumper in terms of providing him with a more effective balancing pole, but there are plenty of first-class jumpers who tend to be short in the neck, often because of their Irish Draught blood. In terms of ability, the length of the back did not seem to have any great impact.

A lot of riders will take the attitude that all this is very interesting, but that what really matters is whether or not a horse leaves the poles untouched. No one would argue with that, but if you are buying an unbroken youngster or aiming to breed show jumpers, conformation characteristics such as these at least give you a little more ammunition.

The way a horse moves can often give a hint as to how he will operate over a fence, although occasionally a horse who scuttles over the ground like a little crab can still manage to power over a big fence. It does not matter so much whether or not a show jumper moves straight, but hopefully he will move from the shoulder in front and from the hips behind, not from the elbow or stifle.

This freedom of movement usually translates into the ability to pick up over fences rather than dangle the lower limbs. In the same way, a lot of people prefer to see a rounder knee action rather than a daisy cutting, show hack type of movement. When you look at the quality of a potential show jumper's paces, concentrate on the canter: as one top rider puts it, 'I've never won any rosettes out of trot.'

The canter should be rhythmic and forward, and many riders prefer a shorter stride to a longer one. Their reasoning is that if you meet the fence wrong on a short striding horse, you will not be so far away from it and will have a better chance of getting to the other side with the poles in place! On the other hand, a horse who is very short striding may find it hard to cope with combinations. Show jumping courses are built to an average canter stride distance of twelve feet and the very short striding horse may get to the final part of a treble and find himself struggling.

A horse's jump starts in his back end, so you will hope to see powerful hindquarters and well-made hocks. All the joints should be flat and hard, as any puffiness shows signs of strain.

If you are buying a horse that has already been broken, you will be able to assess his jumping style over a fence. Seeing him jump loose will not be of any value to you unless you suspect that the rider is restricting the horse's natural ability and in this case, you probably will not want the seller to realise that the horse jumps much better without him! Loose jumping can show you if a young horse has a naturally good style or if, for instance, he tends to dangle a foreleg: the difficulty for the average buyer is that it is very hard to decide whether the problem will sort itself out as the horse muscles up and matures or if it can be corrected through training.

If a horse comes confidently down to a fence with his ears pricked, backs himself off and forms a perfect bascule (arc) over it with feet picked up well out of the way, you have to think you might be on to a good one. If, on the other hand, he needs a lot of encouragement to get to the fence and scrambles over it with a flat back and dangling forelegs, his talents probably lie elsewhere.

Eventing
Eventing is often described as the ultimate challenge for horse and rider. Certainly on paper it looks as if you are asking for the impossible when you look for an event horse:

he has to be calm and obedient for the dressage phase, bold and clean jumping for cross-country and supple and careful for the show jumping phase. In the real world, compromise is often essential as long as you never compromise on soundness.

Boldness and courage are essential attributes for the event horse.

Most event riders will rule out a horse which has had any kind of tendon injury, no matter how good it is in other respects. This may seem unfair when you realise that there are event horses who injure a tendon and eventually return to competition without any more problems, but it is understandable. When so many things can go wrong, why start with the dice loaded against you?

In this sport, priority always used to be put on the cross-country phase and the dressage and show jumping ones came rather a poor second. Whilst cross-country still holds more weight, you can no longer win with a horse who is brilliant cross-country but does a diabolical dressage test or show jumping round. Unless the marking system changes—and there have been suggestions that it should—you still need to be amongst the leaders after the dressage phase. And when the top five are often separated by just a few penalties, a fence or two down in the show jumping can mean the difference between winning and finishing way down the line.

For the top levels of eventing, you inevitably need a horse that is Thoroughbred or near. Much has been made of the fact that warmbloods are making their mark, but when you look at their breeding many of them are actually three-quarters or seven-eighths bred. Their secret weapons are often that they have good movement for the dressage and a level-headed temperament.

But for anyone aiming to compete in pre-novice or novice competitions, a half-bred horse or one of similar type need not be turned down. In fact, their temperaments often makes them easier rides. When you are starting out in this discipline, you do not need to place so much emphasis on a horse's ability to gallop. The best way to avoid time penalties is not to gallop flat out, but to jump out of a rhythm, and that comes from schooling and experience, not racing blood!

The event horse, like the show jumper, must have good limbs and feet. A longer stride is usually thought to be preferable to a short one, but remember that event horses come in all shapes and sizes! Very big horses are often at a disadvantage, and most riders ideally choose something between 16hh and 16.2hh. It is very much a matter of horses for courses, though; the rule book sets the minimum height for an event horse at 15hh, and there have been plenty of good ones who have barely reached the measuring stick.

Although there are some horses over 16.2hh who are as nimble and as athletic as you could wish for, many lack the ability to find an extra leg to get their riders out of trouble, which is so useful in an event horse. They may also find bounces and short distances harder to cope with.

Showing

To those who have not been bitten by the showing bug, it may seem rather like an equine beauty contest with all the emphasis on looks and none on performance. But as ride and manners are an important part of the overall equation, showing classes help to encourage the production of well-made, well-schooled horses which can be no bad thing whatever discipline you are talking about!

A successful show horse needs to have excellent conformation, movement and manners and must also have his fair share of presence: when he goes into the ring he must give the impression of confidence and alertness, as if he is saying 'Look at me.' Never underestimate the importance of a good temperament, because the most beautiful horse in the world will (or should be) at the end of the line if he misbehaves in the ring. He must also be true to type: an elegant show hack is a very different type from a workmanlike cob.

If you are buying a horse to show in a category that requires a height certificate—cobs, small hunters, large and small hacks and large and small riding horses—you must be sure that he has a current height certificate under the Joint Measurement Scheme or that you will be able to get one. Remember that some horses carry on growing until they are five or six, so a four-year-old who is well up to height may not measure in next time. If the horse is seven years or over and has already been registered with the British Show Hack, Cob and Riding Horse Association or National Light Horse Breeding Society, he should hold a life height certificate.

Where height limits apply, the rule books state an upper and lower one: for instance, a cob must be over 14.2hh but not exceed 15.1hh. It has to be said, though, that the horses which do consistently well are those at the upper end of the height limit. If you had two nice cobs who were equal in all respects, but one measured 14.3hh and the other was a full 15.1hh, the larger horse would inevitably get the final nod.

Show hunters

If you want to buy a horse to show in the prestigious weight classes, your horse must be a true lightweight, middleweight or heavyweight. A lightweight is judged as carrying up to 12st 7lb, a middleweight 12st 7lb to 14 stone and a heavyweight 14 stone and over. Showing classes have not yet gone metric! A horse that falls between two categories and is really neither one nor the other will always be at a disadvantage, though could be suitable for ladies' or working hunter classes.

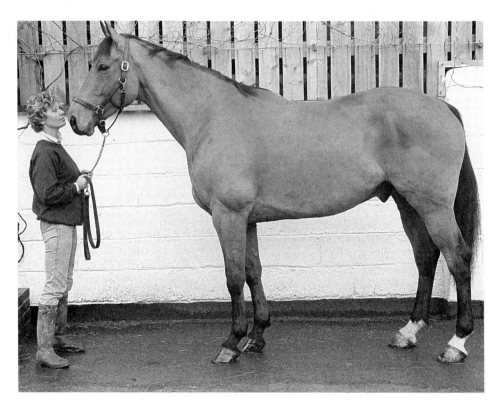

A middleweight show hunter who performs as well in the hunting field as he does in the show ring.

A hunter should be a workmanlike but quality horse with movement to match and good bone: a lightweight should have eight and a half to nine inches of bone, a middleweight nine to nine and half inches and a heavyweight nine and a half inches plus, with everything else in proportion. He should not have the low, daisy cutting paces of a show hack, but he should move straight and true. He must also be able to gallop; this is a horse that the judge should feel happy to hunt on all day.

A lot of show hunters are half or three-quarters Thoroughbred, with the remaining percentage being Irish Draught or occasionally Cleveland Bay. Warmbloods and warmblood cross Thoroughbreds are also making their mark. If you are lucky enough to find a full Thoroughbred who is a true lightweight or middleweight with conformation and temperament to match, you have an outstanding animal.

The small hunter should be the pattern of a miniature middleweight and must stand over 14.2hh but not exceed 15.2hh. Working hunters must be over 15hh and should combine jumping ability with good conformation and paces: these classes are judged 60 per cent on jumping (performance and style) and 40 per cent on ride and conformation.

Hacks

The show hack must be the ultimate in grace, elegance and lightness—a light, well mannered and comfortable ride who never pulls, leans on the bit or misbehaves. As with any show horse, he must move straight but, whereas the hunter and cob have workmanlike actions, the hack should point his toe and have very little knee action.

A show hack should present a picture of grace and elegance.

There are no weight limits in hack classes, but these are basically lightweight horses, although they must never be weedy. The best hacks are usually Thoroughbred or Anglo-Arab, with quality limbs and fine heads. They are divided into two categories, small and large: a small hack must be over 14.2hh but not exceed 15hh, whilst his large counterpart needs to be over 15hh but not more than 15.3hh.

Riding horses

The riding horse is in many ways a cross between a lightweight hunter and a show hack. The hack may be a prettier type, but the riding horse must still be full of quality even though he is more workmanlike and able to gallop.

Three-quarter breds and Anglo-Arabs often do well in these classes, as does the right type of Thoroughbred. They are very popular with amateur owner riders because they are such versatile horses, but as plenty of professionals compete in this class, a good riding horse with a competition record will be as relatively expensive as any other category of show horse.

Again, there are height limits but no weight categories. Small riding horses must be over 14.2hh but not exceed 15.2hh and large ones must be 15.2hh and over.

Cobs

Cobs are the ultimate fun horses and have become incredibly popular over the past few years. The downside of this is that made show cobs or ones with known potential have become very expensive. However, there is always the chance that you can spot the potential of a hairy beast out in a field who has a much lower price tag.

The difference between a show cob and an ordinary cob is sheer quality. A good show cob is powerful and workmanlike, but never common: the old adage is that he should have a head like a duchess and a backside like a cook! Although relatively small in terms of height, over 14.2hh but not exceeding 15.1hh, cobs are so powerful and deep through the girth that they can take almost any rider.

Lightweight cobs should be able to carry riders of up to 14 stone and heavyweights are up to 14 stone or over. It is very important that their limbs match their bodies: a lightweight cob must have a minimum of eight and a half inches of bone and a heavyweight needs nine inches plus.

Although they must give a comfortable ride, which means that they must not be too straight in the shoulder or have a driving type knee action, cobs should not be plods. A true show cob will be able to show an impressive gallop.

Most cobs are naturally good jumpers, thanks to their powerful back ends. A cob who can compete successfully in open working cob classes, which are judged in a similar format to those for working hunters, will have the ability to jump a Discovery class under British Show Jumping Association rules.

Many of the best show cobs have unknown breeding, though there are now cob breeding classes in the same way as there are for hunters and hacks. A lot have a high percentage of Irish Draught blood and some are actually pure Irish Draught.

Endurance

The popularity of endurance riding has soared over the past few years. Once thought of, both patronisingly and inaccurately, as suitable for middle-aged ladies who enjoy a quiet poddle round the countryside, it is now recognised as a challenging sport that demands a true partnership of horse and rider. Non-competitive pleasure rides average about ten miles, whilst competitive rides start at 20 miles and go up to the ultimate test, namely 100 mile rides such as the Golden Horseshoe or even tougher. For the really ambitious who are prepared to ride on the international circuit, there are ultimate challenges such as desert marathon races and rides through the USA's most challenging territories.

Most riders who aim to take the sport seriously go for either a pure-bred Arab or a horse with predominantly Arab blood. This is because the Arab has been bred through generations for stamina, agility and ground-covering movement—all essential attributes for endurance. However, there are exceptions to what too many riders look on as a hard and fast rule: Jackie Taylor's Sally, one of the most successful endurance horses of recent years, is Trakehner cross Anglo-Arab with only 25 per cent Arab blood. Joy Loyla's Hero, a member of Britain's gold medal winning endurance team at the Stockholm World Equestrian Games, is a tough little palomino of unknown breeding whose owner turned to endurance riding in a desperate bid to improve his difficult temperament!

There are many stories of horses who have been condemned as difficult or impossible rides finding their niche in endurance riding, perhaps because they thrive on plenty of work. An endurance horse has got to want to keep going as much as his rider does. A lot of hotheads settle to it because so much is involved in both the fittening work and the actual competitions, although that does not mean every problem horse is a future endurance star!

Good feet and limbs are vital for the endurance horse. He has to carry himself and his rider over all sorts of terrain, including stony tracks, and weaknesses such as flat feet and thin soles are soon found out. He must also have a natural athleticism, agility and balance; the endurance horse is not asked to go on the bit, but must be in balance. He is often ridden on a loose rein and his head and neck conformation must give him an efficient balancing pole.

Most endurance horses are around 15hh, though there is no reason why a bigger horse cannot do well if it has all the other necessary attributes. It is also particularly important that his owner/rider likes him because they will have to spend a lot of time together!

The first horse or pony and the schoolmaster

The first horse or pony needs to know a lot more than his rider, but have a generous enough temperament not to take advantage of him—quite a tall order. By definition, he has been there, seen it and done it all, which means that he is usually seven or over. There are a few gems who are rock steady and perfect at four or five, but they are few and far between. For this reason, you may find that an older horse, including one up to his early teens, is a good bet. This is especially true of ponies, many of whom stay fit and sound well into their twenties.

Obviously there are minuses as well as pluses to buying an older, experienced animal—the main ones are that he may be showing signs of wear and tear and may be difficult to sell if or when his rider is ready for something more challenging. A veterinary examination will take care of the first issue, whilst the second is down to you: you may have to accept that you are giving the horse his last home.

There are also plenty of horses described as suitable first time mounts who are nothing of the sort. Unfortunately a lot of people think a bone idle animal with an insensitive mouth and sides is suitable for a beginner because the hapless rider cannot do any harm. He might not do any harm, but neither will he achieve anything—he will either be totally disheartened by having to pull on the reins and kick the animal in the ribs or assume that this is the way every horse or pony needs to be ridden.

A first pony must be safe and reliable. Kitty is a paragon of virtue who has helped several children learn to ride.

There may be grounds for not choosing a particularly sensitive mount for a first horse, however steady and obedient he is with a competent rider, because he will perhaps be confused by a rider who is not always perfectly balanced. However, he must be responsive enough to do the right thing if the rider presses the right buttons. He must also be good in traffic, to catch, shoe and handle. Ideally he will also be good to clip and box, though these are problems that can often be overcome with experienced help if the animal is perfect in every other respect.

Looks are not usually important in themselves, though you do not want a horse or pony whose conformation makes him an uncomfortable ride. The commonest problems with older animals are arthritis and those related to concussion, such as navicular syndrome and ringbone (which are now thought to have an arthritic link as well). Again, your vet will help you weigh up the pros and cons.

First horses and ponies are often described as schoolmasters, but the true schoolmaster or mistress is a very different proposition. This is an animal that has been schooled to a high standard, perhaps in dressage or show jumping, and is straightforward enough to be ridden by someone starting out in a particular discipline and wanting to specialise in it. It may be a horse who has reached a certain level, albeit fairly high, and who will not go any farther but has a valuable role teaching competent riders who want to go farther the correct feel.

The true schoolmaster is hard to find and may be comparatively expensive. He will almost certainly need regular re-tuning by an expert rider to keep him established in his work. However, as long as he is sound he will never be hard to place in a new home.

Ponies (also see previous section)

Buying ponies is perhaps even more complicated than buying horses because three people are now involved: the vendor, the purchaser—usually a parent—and the child. Very often parents looking for ponies for their children have little or no knowledge of ponies; they think that the child knows enough, and the child may share that opinion. This sort of situation leads to trouble, so the first step for an inexperienced parent is to get expert help.

Ask your child's riding instructor to help, providing that they have plenty of practical knowledge, or contact the district commissioner of your local Pony Club branch. The Pony Club has an amazing parents' network and word soon gets round of good, outgrown ponies who are looking for new homes.

There are a few golden rules with buying ponies. The first is never to match an inexperienced child with an inexperienced (which usually means young) pony. They will not, as many parents fondly imagine, learn together. What usually happens is that the rider becomes confused or frightened and the pony ends up in the same state, often obtaining a bad reputation that he does not deserve.

Another mistake is to buy a pony bigger than the child can manage in the expectation that they will grow into it. A child cannot control a pony that is too big and strong and may end up frightened or worse. Similarly, you should not necessarily take your child's word on their riding ability—many youngsters think they are better than they are, and riding a lively pony under supervision is very different from coping with him alone.

It might seem like a good idea to ask if your local riding school has anything suitable for sale. In practice, good riding school ponies are worth their weight in gold and are rarely sold. If they do come on the market, perhaps because a school closes down, you may run into problems at first if you buy one.

Riding school ponies can become a bit institutionalised. They work hard, much harder than the average animal in private ownership, and are nearly always ridden in company. Take them away and ask them to work on their own for a fraction of the time and you may find you have a confused pony who says 'Won't.'

The riding club horse

The riding club horse is a Jack of all Trades who is competent at most things. He may well excel at show jumping or dressage, but should also be able to complete an unaffiliated one-day event with a good mark in each discipline. He can be any height, colour or breed as long as he suits his rider; there are more than 600 riding clubs affiliated to the British Horse Society in Britain, and at any of their competitions you will see animals ranging from native ponies to Thoroughbreds, with every possible variation in between.

An ideal riding club type is probably a nice, workmanlike half-bred horse. He should present a pleasing overall picture and move well enough to give a comfortable ride at all paces. Even if he is green, you should feel that with a bit more schooling he would be capable of doing a nice preliminary or unaffiliated novice dressage test. Likewise, he should have the character and scope to jump a three foot three to three foot six course. Many riding club members are not interested in competing on the affiliated circuit but having said that, there are a lot of riders who get the taste for competing at club level and decide to have a go at affiliated level.

Above all, the riding club horse is one to have fun with and who will try everything. He is the sort of animal a lot of people are looking for.

The family ride and drive animal

The family ride and drive horse or pony is similar to the riding club horse in that he needs to be a good all-rounder; the difference is that he is just at home in harness as he is under saddle and is suitable for riders of different ages. His height and build will enable him to carry a competent child—though not a real tiny—and their parent, so you are inevitably looking at a native or native cross, perhaps an Irish or Welsh cob.

He must be good on the roads and be a reasonably well-schooled ride. You might have to compromise and accept that a good driving animal could have a slightly choppy stride under saddle; his trot will probably be faster than a riding cob and canter will not usually be his best natural pace. Despite that, some animals have an uncanny knack of adapting their way of going to whatever job they are doing: their owners are the lucky ones!

A horse or pony that is well broken to harness should be responsive to the voice. If you hit problems, all you have to do is say 'Whoa', which is a salutary reminder to us all of how important the voice commands are and how we should ensure that every horse responds to them. When riding, be prepared for him to want to position himself more in the middle of the road than at the side: this is the position he is used to when being driven and may expect to stick to it.

Ex-racehorses

Many people are attracted to the idea of buying an ex-racehorse, often because they are relatively cheap; it quite possible to buy one for under £1,000. But before taking one on, it is important to realise that they present special problems and considerations that must be taken into account: you may find that your bargain horse turns out to be an expensive buy in both financial and emotional terms.

Of all the thousands of horses bred for racing each year, only a tiny percentage actually make the grade. The rest become racing rejects, either because they are simply not fast enough or because they have soundness problems. The first does not matter but the second obviously does.

The commonest problems are those relating to legs—notably tendon strain—and backs. These horses are backed as yearlings and raced before they are physically or mentally mature: admittedly they carry lightweight riders, but it is still a lot for them to cope with.

Racehorses are inevitably sold at auction through specialised bloodstock sales; in Britain, the main venues are Newmarket, Ascot, Doncaster and Malvern. Racing people look on this as the accepted and most convenient way of buying and selling, but buying at auction is not for the inexperienced (see Chapter 6). You will not be able to ride the horse, so it will have to be assessed purely on the grounds of what is before you.

There are good dealers who buy at auction, re-school the horses and then sell them on. The work and time put into these horses will obviously make them more expensive than horses bought straight out of training but in the long term, it can work out cheaper. The risks will have already been taken and you will be able to try the horse and have it vetted just like any other.

If you are attracted by the idea of a Thoroughbred, never turn down an ex-racehorse just because it has raced. If it has stayed sound through training and accepted a new way of life, it often has a lot going for it.

Many people consider ex-racehorses to be hot-headed with no brakes, but that is not true. They are as much individuals as other horses and some can be remarkably sensible, though you will still be buying a highly bred horse with quick reactions.

You may think that you can buy a three-year-old out of training, get on it and turn it into a show jumper/eventer or whatever in a relatively short time. Professionals can and do, but most turn their horses out for a while to relax, and learn how to be an ordinary horse. Racehorses are stabled for twenty-two or twenty-three hours a day which is why there is a higher than average incidence of stable vices, another issue to consider. Giving them time in the field takes the edge off their fitness.

They are broken and ridden in a different way from other horses. The trainer's main aim is, after all, to produce a horse that gallops faster than all the others; most are not bothered about whether a horse bends evenly or what sort of head carriage it adopts. They are ridden by lightweight riders who adopt very short stirrups: a racehorse will not be familiar with orthodox leg aids and will certainly not know how to move away from the leg.

Because they are broken and ridden at a time when they are continually cutting teeth, many tend to be unsettled in their mouths. Correct riding and bitting can overcome this, but it takes time and patience. Racehorses are usually ridden in loose ring snaffles, but unfortunately a lot of yards put any bridle on any horse and you frequently see racehorses in bits that are too big and incorrectly adjusted.

Many racehorses are used to traffic, which is a bonus. However, they are nearly always ridden out to the gallops in a string, with horses going nose to tail. Again, it takes time and patience to get them used to going out and working alone: nappiness, which in this case is the horse's way of showing that he is insecure, is common.

You have to be prepared to treat most racehorses as just backed youngsters and go right back to basics with them: lungeing, long reining and so on. The exception may be the ex-point-to-point horse who has been hunted as part of the qualification process; he will be older and have had a more varied lifestyle.

Thoroughbreds have thin skins and fine coats, which makes them susceptible to the weather. They usually need plenty of food and rugs, and are therefore more expensive to keep in autumn and winter than, say, a half-bred horse. That said, some people love them and find them the most rewarding type of horse to work with.

Hunters

In many ways the ordinary hunter should have similar characteristics to the show and working hunter. He must be a bold, well-mannered ride who can carry you safely over your chosen country, with a jumping ability to match. But whereas a successful show hunter will have textbook conformation, his counterpart in the real world need not be judged so stringently as long as there is nothing that prejudices his soundness. Many show hunters never go cross-country or see a fence, let alone a pack of hounds; there are a few that do, but they are definitely in the minority.

There is a big difference in the demands made by different types of country. On Exmoor, for instance, a horse required to follow staghounds can go all day without meeting a fence, whereas one following the Quorn will need considerable jumping and galloping ability. Both must have good manners: a horse which refuses to stand still or which kicks at other horses or hounds is a liability.

A horse that has hunted well for several seasons may show a few signs of wear and tear, such as scars and splints. As long as your vet is happy that they will have no detriment on his soundness, you can disregard them.

A hunter must be a suitable stamp of horse for his rider. This may sound obvious, but you would not usually want to choose a strong 16.2hh middleweight when you are five foot two and eight stone. Cobs often make remarkably good hunters, as they frequently combine weight carrying ability with jumping prowess and calm temperaments: if well schooled, they can be as light to ride as any other sort of horse.

A hunter does not have to be a particular breed, height or colour, but he must be the sort of horse you are happy to ride all day. It is important that he is up to your weight because, no matter how small and lightweight are, you are going to be on his back for a long period. At the end of a long day, when you are both tired, your horse needs something in reserve—so aim for a horse that can comfortably carry a stone more than your weight.

Look for chest room and plenty of depth through the girth, which should denote stamina, but unless you are really tall do not necessarily go for a really big horse. A well-made, up to weight 15.2–16.1hh should be handy enough to cope with all types of conditions and will also be easier to keep looking well. Big, rangy horses often look like greyhounds at the end of a hard day's hunting; a 17hh Thoroughbred might look impressive standing in his box, but you are buying a horse to do a job, not to show off on.

A well-schooled horse who is balanced and clever is much more pleasant to hunt than one who tanks along on his forehand pulling your arms out; it is important that he keeps these attributes in the open as well as in an enclosed arena. He must be able to gallop, but come back to you as willingly as he goes on, and he must also cope happily with the sort of obstacles you will encounter in the hunting field: ditches, water, hedges, etc.

It is very important that a hunter is good to box. It is bad enough trying to load a reluctant horse on a showground when there are potential helpers around; trying to persuade him up the ramp when you are tired, fed up and parked in a country lane is even worse.

If you are buying a made hunter, he should come complete with a history of his experience in the hunting field, and his owner should not object to you contacting the field master to ask if he knows the horse or has seen him out. Irish horses are almost bound to have hunted because the Irish way of breaking in a horse is to put a saddle on his back and follow hounds!

Ideally, you should look for a horse that has hunted in similar country to your own: a big, galloping Leicestershire hunter may not be half as talented over trappy, up and down country where gallops are few and far between. Similarly, a clever little horse who can find a fifth leg may get left behind over big hedges and open turf.

Hunters are usually advertised for sale from September onwards, as proper hunters as opposed to all-rounders who also hunt are turned away for the summer. There are professional dealers who specialise in hunters, and usually hunt to display their wares. It is obviously a good idea to see a horse performing, as long as you are sure that you are a good enough rider to get the best out of him. Some dealers may let genuine buyers try a horse for half a day in the hunting field, or will offer to exchange him if you do not like him when you have taken him out for the first time.

If you want a horse that has a reasonable amount of experience in the hunting field you are going to be looking at an animal who is at least six years old. Event horses that have reached their limit are sometimes sold as hunters, but they are not necessarily easy rides—and if the horse has reached his limit because, for instance, he was unreliable about jumping ditches he may be just as unsuitable for hunting.

Chapter 4
Breeds and their Characteristics

Over the past few years the interest in how horses are bred has increased. At one time the general attitude was that if an animal had the talent and did the job you wanted, its parentage was irrelevant. Some people may still argue that this applies, but there is an increasing feeling that to get the best, you have to breed from the best and if you know a horse's lineage then you are better placed to spot potential talent.

Results from breeding programmes in Germany, Holland, France and other countries show that breeding from performance lines pays dividends. So whilst at first sight it may not seem to matter how a gelding is bred, because he will not produce any offspring, knowing that he comes from a successful line of jumpers, dressage horses or whatever may give you a head start to success. The British Horse Database aims to give British breeders and buyers the same guidelines to assessing potential as those available on the Continent.

Britain has a wealth of horse and pony breeds, and there are many others from the Continent and farther afield who are proving themselves in all disciplines. You may find yourself drawn to a particular breed or type and want to own a pure-bred because you like its looks and characteristics. Even if you are not particularly bothered, physical and temperamental characteristics can be so strong that knowing a horse's breeding can give you an idea of its likely strengths and weaknesses.

As horses are as individual as people, there is no such thing as a stereotype Arab, Thoroughbred or whatever. Outside factors such as environment and how well or badly the horse has been handled and ridden before you buy him are just as important. And remembering that breeds originated to do particular jobs may help you to decide what sort of animal to look for.

Although this chapter takes a wide-ranging look at breeds and their characteristics, it does not claim to be comprehensive. To discuss every breed would take a book in its own, and there are plenty available. We have tried to be fair, but the chapter is inevitably coloured by the authors' experience so whilst we have found that many Cleveland Bay crosses can have a stubborn streak, do not take that as an iron-clad certainty. There are also plenty of horses bred this way who are as co-operative as you could wish for.

Just to make life even more complicated, many top riders swear that the horses that are the most difficult to start with turn out to be the biggest stars. Those with an independent streak may have an innate ability to think for themselves, which, if channelled correctly, can be a great help when the going gets tough—for instance, the horse that can help you out if you meet a fence wrong has the advantage over the one who meets it wrong and goes through it, or worse!

However, the big if with this type of horse is whether its rider has the temperament, ability and time to steer its independence in the right direction. It is all very well having a horse who is up to the challenges you want to set him, but remember that it is equally important that you are up to any challenges he may set you!

Horse breeds

Arab

An animal up to 14.2hh is usually a pony and one over that height a horse, but an Arab is officially a horse whatever its size. It is a breed that people either love or hate and rarely inspires half measures.

Arabs tend to be lightweight and have good, flat bone (see Chapter 2). For most, the natural way of going is with a high head and tail carriage; they can be difficult to get on the bit, simply because their conformation sometimes makes it hard for them. Their high tail carriage may also give the optical illusion that they are not rounding over their backs and working through from behind, even when they are doing just that. Some dressage and showing judges (except those in the breed showing classes) are prejudiced against them, which can be disheartening.

The Arab's stamina makes him the perfect mount for top level endurance riding.

Arabs have plenty of stamina, but some tend to be scatty rather than sensitive. How much of that is inherent in the breed and how much is caused by incorrect handling is debatable; there has been a tendency, particularly in the show ring, for handlers to deliberately wind up their horses to give them extra presence. Fortunately, many Arab enthusiasts frown on this and their views now appear to carry more weight.

Arabs are often ideal for endurance riding, but are usually not natural jumpers. As always, there are exceptions to the rule, including pure-bred Arabs who compete successfully in dressage, eventing and show jumping. Inevitably this is at the lower levels of affiliated competition, but that may be perfectly sufficient for most riders.

Although they are strong for their size and can be very athletic, Arabs are usually fairly small, which can be a drawback for tall riders. Most are in the 14.2–15.1hh range and it is rare to find one of 15.2hh or over. Some of those that top the average height range tend to be over long in the leg.

Arab enthusiasts say that these are real one-to-one horses. They need owners who are prepared to build up relationships with them and who have the time and ability to treat them as individuals. Ideally, of course, the same applies to all horses and ponies.

Anglo-Arab

The Anglo-Arab is half or three-quarters Thoroughbred and the remainder is Arab blood. The part-bred Arab is at least a quarter Arab and the rest may be any breed except Thoroughbred. Arab cross Welsh is a favourite combination, but you may come across many others.

There are many good show horses that are Anglos; they tend to combine the good movement of the Arab with the elegance of the Thoroughbred, and often have good temperaments. Although all generalisations to do with horses are dangerous, Anglos tend to make their mark in the dressage and showing worlds rather than in show jumping or eventing.

Arab blood has a very strong influence and a horse who is only a quarter Arab may still show many characteristics—in particular, a higher than usual tail carriage and a pretty head with a dished face.

Cleveland Bay

The Cleveland Bay is basically a driving horse and, as its name suggests, is always bay in colour. It tends to be a little upright in the shoulder, which makes for an efficient driving horse but gives a more up and down action and a less comfortable ride. They can also tend to be straighter than is desirable in the hind leg, which can predispose them to hock problems.

The pure-bred Cleveland Bay is few in number and is often crossed with the Thoroughbred to produce sport horses for the riding world. An infusion of Thoroughbred blood often gives a more sloping shoulder and thus better movement for riding.

The Cleveland Bay is officially a rare breed, but a strong band of enthusiasts should ensure its future. There is a recognition that many breeders will want to ensure that part-bred Clevelands have the conformation that makes a good riding horse, and that there is perhaps less demand for those with pure driving characteristics. That is not to say that the Cleveland Bay is not in demand for driving. He makes a supreme carriage horse, and has a strong presence in the Royal Mews.

Irish Draught

The Irish Draught is a workhorse, but crossed with the Thoroughbred gives one of the best combinations. They are usually laid-back, with level temperaments, and are often talented jumpers. Conformation pluses usually include good feet and limbs and powerful hindquarters, but they can sometimes be a bit straight in the shoulder—though modern breeders have done a lot to get rid of this fault. The three-quarter Thoroughbred, quarter Irish Draught will have rounder bone (see Chapter 2) and more quality.

The Irish Draught/Thoroughbred cross or the three-quarter Thoroughbred, quarter Irish Draught usually has a natural agility and the ability to find a fifth leg when necessary, which is extremely useful for a hunter or show jumper.

Quarter Horse

The Quarter Horse was originally bred as an American workhorse, where his compact, powerful build coupled with athleticism made him ideal for everything from working cattle to light draught work. He quickly became an animal to have fun with, too: he was raced over quarter mile distances, hence his name.

A Thoroughbred mare straight out of racing.

Today the versatile Quarter Horse is still used for racing; Quarter Horse racing offers good prizes and an atmosphere and camaraderie that enthusiasts believe cannot be matched. But he is also used for Western riding and for every discipline under English saddle, from dressage to show jumping.

Characteristics include a deep girth, powerful hindquarters and sloping pasterns. Like the Thoroughbred, his neck tends to be set slightly low—when a horse works cattle, he needs to be able to stretch his neck and have the freedom to use it as a balancing pole, with his rider using weight and neck reining aids. Again, this can make it theoretically more difficult for the horse to work with a higher head carriage, but correct training and riding coupled with the Quarter Horse's willing temperament mean it is not usually a problem.

Average height is around 15–15.2hh, but there are many larger examples of the breed. Some people cross them with Thoroughbreds, but the breed has enough quality and athleticism of its own.

Thoroughbred

The Thoroughbred is one of the most influential breeds in the world and imparts quality to whatever it is crossed with. The pure Thoroughbred has been described as the ultimate horse, but while it can excel in any discipline it was bred first and foremost to race.

The same mare after she had been turned out and let down.

A Thoroughbred is naturally designed to go long, low and as fast as possible. That does not mean he cannot work on the bit and achieve a high degree of collection, but it does not come as naturally to him as it does to a breed such as the warmblood. Most advanced event horses are either Thoroughbred or seven-eighths bred because they possess the necessary speed, stamina and courage.

Many Thoroughbreds are ex-racehorses, which can lead to them having particular problems and may rule them out as being suitable for the average rider (see Chapter 3). They are not suitable for anyone who needs a horse that can live out all the time, as they are too thin skinned. They usually need twice as much food and twice as many rugs as horses with cold blood, which means they are not cheap to keep.

Warmblood

Warmblood is an overall term used to describe Continental horses, all of which are a mixture of Thoroughbred and cold-blooded horses. You can get German, Swedish, Dutch and Danish warmbloods, either bred in their country of origin and brought over here or bred in Britain.

The Continentals have a much better breeding programme than exists at present in Britain, although in recent years the British Horse Database has started to rectify that and good warmbloods fetch fabulous prices abroad for dressage or show jumping. Unfortunately they have become fashionable, and sadly we tend to get a lot of imported second-class horses because they are cheaper. There are, however, many good ones bred in this country.

Good warmbloods have done well in dressage and show jumping and can be crossed successfully with the Thoroughbred. Their drawbacks are a tendency to narrow, boxy feet and in some cases, the need for constant reinforcement of schooling. Those who like them call them laid-back, those who do not say they are thick!

Many modern warmbloods have a high percentage of Thoroughbred blood, to the extent that they will be three-quarter or even seven-eighths bred. This has made them lighter and more athletic; the modern Hanoverian, for instance, is very different from the huge, rather cumbersome beast of a few years ago. As one leading dressage rider puts it, today's warmbloods are athletes rather than dancing elephants!

The heavy breeds

If you feel that heavy horse breeds are out of place in a book that is concerned primarily with riding animals, then think again. Clydesdale, Shire or Suffolk Punch cross Thoroughbred are becoming increasingly popular as hunters and show jumpers. The three-quarter Thoroughbred, quarter heavy horse is perhaps even more suited to the competition world.

Crossing horses so dramatically different in type seems to have one of two results. If you are lucky, you get the best of both worlds: a horse that combines quality, substance, a nice temperament and a powerful jump. If you are unlucky, the result can be an animal with a big head and a front end that does not match the back.

The heavy horse breeds are all big, but the Shire is the one most people think of when talking about the giants of the horse world. They are usually over 16.2hh—sometimes a hand taller—and can weigh well over a ton. Their relatively long necks and sloping shoulders make them a good cross, inevitably with a Thoroughbred, to produce a substantial riding horse: some owners do actually ride their Shires. A band of them were once the most memorable part of a film: they were cast as the mounts of primitive Man, which involved rather a lot of poetic licence!

Clydesdales are lighter and usually slightly smaller than Shires. They often have plenty of white markings; long stockings, blazes and white on the belly are common, and they often pass these on to their offspring.

The Suffolk Punch is the oldest of the British heavy horse breeds and has a unique characteristic—it is always chestnut. Unlike the Shire and the Clydesdale, it has hardly any feather. The three-quarter Thoroughbred, quarter Suffolk Punch cross often seems to produce horses with a natural talent for jumping.

Pony breeds

Britain's pony breeds are the envy of the world and combine good temperaments with hardiness. They are very versatile and the larger breeds, such as Connemaras and Welsh Section Ds, can make admirable mounts for all but the largest adults. If you want an animal to have lots of fun with and are working to a budget, a native pony could be a good buy. They are happiest living out all or most of the time, which fits in well with the lifestyles of many working owners, and are cheap to feed.

Native ponies can and do compete on equal terms with horses in dressage and other competitions. Recently, Connemara, Highland and New Forest ponies have done well in affiliated dressage.

The only drawback for the adult rider is that many open show jumping competitions place an age limit on pony riders. This means that you need to either find yourself a pony that measures over 14.2hh or compete in mountain and moorland working hunter classes instead of show jumping.

Some riders, of course, do not want to compete at all. If your priorities are a pleasant, well-schooled ride, an enjoyable hack and/or a mount for sponsored rides, a native pony could again fit the bill. There must be one word of warning, though: top class ponies, particularly representatives of the larger breeds, fetch high prices.

The larger native ponies are often crossed with Thoroughbreds and the result is often a small horse that combines quality with a fair amount of hardiness and pony common sense. The most popular crosses are the Connemara and Welsh Section D cross Thoroughbred. The average size of first cross animals is 15–16hh, though there are plenty who end up taller: Penarth Blue Steel, a successful Welsh Cob cross Thoroughbred show jumper and working hunter, stands 16.2hh.

Many event riders like a horse who is nearly Thoroughbred but has a small percentage—perhaps one-eighth or one-sixteenth—native blood. They feel, often with justification, that the dash of pony breeding gives a handiness and the natural ability to jump itself out of trouble.

Connemara

Connemara ponies originate, not surprisingly, from Ireland and combine quality with substance. Their heights range officially from 13–14.2hh, but sometimes a pony will go over height and reach 15hh. Although this will preclude him from being shown in breed classes, he would still make a very nice small horse! Some over height Connemaras have been successful in 15hh working hunter pony classes or even as show cobs.

A four-year-old Connemara cross Thoroughbred who has the potential to do many jobs.

Unlike some native breeds, the Connemara has been bred to produce a good riding pony. They usually have a nice sloping shoulder and a good length of rein, and so ride big: in other words, you feel as if you are mounted on a small horse rather than a pony. Although some tend to be slightly long in the back, this is acceptable in the breed; they were originally bred to carry panniers and a rider.

Most Connemaras have powerful hindquarters and a natural talent for jumping. They have quality heads and are clean through the throat and jawline, and so with correct schooling they find it easy to work on the bit.

Dales
Dales and Fell ponies share many common characteristics and even experts may sometimes be hard put to tell the difference between the two. Breed guidelines mean that the Dales pony is slightly larger, up to 14.2hh and heavier.

He is strong and up to weight, with a strong, short back and a powerful trot. A Dales pony will be cheap on farrier's bills, as he has very tough, hard feet and can often be worked unshod.

Dartmoor

Dartmoor ponies make lovely riding ponies for children, but as their maximum height is 12.2hh they are too small for most adults. Like the Connemara, they have good shoulders and length of rein, which again makes for a comfortable ride.

The Dartmoor makes a superb children's pony.

The Dartmoor's ride is enhanced by the way he moves: he shows very little knee action and usually has a long stride for his size.

Exmoor

The Exmoor is the oldest British pony breed and also one of the rarest. At present there are only about 800 in the world, which makes them rarer than the giant panda.

Exmoor enthusiasts have a fierce determination to keep them true to the original type, whilst the other breeds have evolved to suit riders' demands. This means that in many ways, they are at a disadvantage; their necks are heavily muscled underneath and they are often straighter in the shoulder than is desirable in textbook terms for riding conformation.

These ponies are very strong and can carry up to eleven stone. However, their small height—the breed society maximum is 12.2hh for mares and 12.3hh for geldings and stallions—means that most adult riders find their feet are rather too close to the ground for comfort.

Fell

At first sight the Fell pony looks very like the Dales: powerful, with generous feathers (fine, silky hair at the heels). However, they are slightly smaller—the maximum height for a Fell pony according to the breed standard is 14hh—and sometimes have a more sloping shoulder.

Like Dales ponies, Fells are up to weight and will take an adult rider quite happily. Both breeds have kind temperaments and are popular trekking mounts.

Highland

Highland ponies are real powerhouses. Although they should not exceed 14.2hh, they are strong and hardy. They were bred to carry deer carcasses weighing fifteen stone or even more; this weight-carrying ability, coupled with the Highland's depth through the girth, means he can easily carry a large man.

Highland ponies are up to a lot of weight.

The Highland cross Thoroughbred is not one of the commonest crosses, but can produce a nice all-round riding horse. If the first cross is again crossed with the Thoroughbred, the result can be a quality horse with a useful sure-footedness. There have been several successful event horses who have had a touch of Highland blood.

New Forest

New Forest ponies make ideal mounts for children and small adults. Good specimens are very different from the scrubby ponies often seen wandering around the area, though steps have been taken recently to improve their condition. Foresters range from around 13–14.2hh, and should be deep through the girth with a sloping shoulder.

The New Forest is a popular riding pony.

This breed has a longer, lower action than some native breeds, but its representatives are just as sure-footed.

Shetland

The Shetland is the smallest of the native pony breeds and is measured in inches rather than hands. The average height is around 38–40 inches; miniature Shetlands are even smaller, but their value must be questioned. What is the point of breeding ponies too small even for children to ride?

Shetlands are very strong. They were bred to carry heavy weights and could in theory be ridden by a big adult (though such a person would probably need roller skates as well). They have an often undeserved reputation for being stroppy: if they are handled correctly and treated as ponies rather than spoiled pets, they are just as well behaved as any other breed.

The Shetland is the smallest of the native breeds.

Crossing a Shetland with a Thoroughbred does not bear thinking about. As far as we know, no one has attempted it or thought of a reason to do so!

Welsh

The Welsh breeds are divided into four sections: Section A is the Welsh Mountain Pony, Section B the Welsh Pony, Section C the Welsh pony of cob type and Section D the Welsh Cob. Heights range from an upper limit of 12hh for the Section A to 15hh or over for the Section D.

All the Welsh breeds have presence, that 'look at me' quality that makes them stand out from the crowd. The Section C and Section D are both capable of carrying adults; in fact the Section D is really a small horse with pony character. If you are thinking of buying a Welsh Cob as a riding horse, choose one with a riding rather than a driving action—they all have a round knee action, but some are too up and down in their movement to be comfortable under saddle.

The Welsh Cob cross Thoroughbred or three-quarters Thoroughbred, quarter Welsh Cob is a popular type for competition. Welsh Cobs are often talented jumpers and a number of part-breds have been successful eventers.

The Welsh Section A combines beauty and strength.

The Welsh Section B is another beautiful pony who makes a good mount for children. Welsh ponies are also popular with driving enthusiasts.

The Welsh Cob (Section D) is the biggest and most powerful of the Welsh breeds.

When crossed with the Thoroughbred, the Welsh Cob often produces a quality horse with a powerful jump.

Chapter 5
Other Factors

The penultimate areas to think about before you look at the adverts are age, sex, colour and whether or not you are prepared to tolerate any stable vices. The final issue is price! Although these subjects have already been touched on, they deserve more than a cursory glance.

Age

If you could pick a magic age that would appeal to most horse buyers, it would probably be six or seven. The reason is that at this stage in its life, a young animal has seen enough of life to have gained experience but has plenty of years ahead of it. As

All foals are cute and cuddly. But will he grow into the type of horse you need?

always, there are a lot of provisos behind this somewhat rash statement. To be worth a premium price, the horse must have been educated correctly and not pushed too hard, too soon. By the same yardstick, he must not have learned or been forced into any bad habits such as napping or rearing and he must be sound.

Most dealers will tell you that the most sought after horse, and therefore inevitably the most expensive one, is the animal aged between five and eight. If your budget is limited, it may be necessary to give yourself more choice by looking outside that age range. Both younger and older horses have a lot to offer, and may be the first choice of many buyers, but there are considerations to be taken into account.

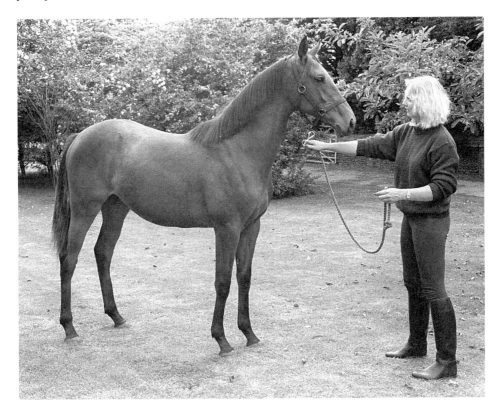

If you buy a yearling, remember that it will be at least two years before you can think of starting to break him in.

Many people love the idea of bringing on a young horse, whether they set their sights on a newly weaned foal, an unbroken yearling, two or three-year-old or a four-year-old with that magic word, potential. If budget restrictions are your reason for buying a youngster, you might want do a few sums and then perhaps think again!

A weanling may be cheap to buy; his price will probably be calculated in terms of hundreds rather than thousands, unless he has such an illustrious ancestry that his eventual value could be many times that. If his breeder has paid a four-figure stud fee and has also shouldered the cost of veterinary care and feed for the pregnant mare and her offspring, he is going to want something extra for his time and the risks taken. Even in a depressed market, no breeder wants to breed at a loss even though breeding for profit may not always be easy—there is an old saying that fools breed horses for wise men to ride!

A horse costs roughly the same amount of money to keep whether he is six months old or four years old. If he is to stand the best chance of growing up strong and healthy, he needs the right food, shelter and attention from your vet and farrier. Obviously he will not need to be shod until starting his ridden career, but his feet still need trimming every four to six weeks and he still needs worming, vaccinating and teeth checks/rasping.

To keep him until he can be backed at three and start his proper work at four means an awful lot of paying out, especially if you keep him in some kind of livery set-up. When he is ready to break, you need the right set-up to do it safely and efficiently; if you do not have the experience or the confidence to do it yourself, you will have to send him to a professional to do it for you and pay a suitable sum for their expertise.

Backing a youngster takes time, manpower, experience and the right facilities.

Backing and bringing on a youngster demands lots of time and good facilities. There will often be times when you need to give him two short lessons a day rather than one long one and if you need to work through a problem, you do not want to give up on a confused or stroppy horse because you have to leave for work. A safe, enclosed area for lungeing, introducing long reining and those first lessons under saddle is also necessary. It must have safe fencing and a good footing, which by definition usually means an outdoor manege.

No one can train a young horse alone: it is neither practical nor safe. There are times when you need someone to hold and reassure him while you introduce him to new experiences, such as wearing rugs or getting used to the feel of long reins. If you do not have a reliable helper who is available whenever needed, you do have problems.

All this is not meant to put you off. If you can satisfy the above criteria and do not mind waiting before you have a chance to ride your young horse, it can be a very rewarding experience. It can also teach you just how much we take for granted when handling older horses and how trusting most young animals are if they are always treated fairly and kindly.

You do not need to be a top-class rider to take on a youngster, but you do need to have the right temperament. Those with short fuses rarely make a good job of it and neither do the sentimentalists. Good trainers apply patience, kindness, firmness and common sense in equal doses. You also need to be a reasonable rider possessing a balanced seat, a clear idea of what aids to apply and when, the ability to ride and handle a horse in a consistent fashion and the knack of keeping things as simple as possible.

This may sound as if it is turning into one of those Catch 22 situations—a bit like looking for work and being forever told that you do not have the experience for the job and no one will give you the chance to gain it. There are two ways round it, though.

First, if you have the money and can find someone willing to break your horse and put up with you at the same time, send him to a sympathetic professional who will let you become involved with the process. This may be easier said than done because a lot of trainers like to do things their own way in their own time without someone in the background asking questions all the time. This does not mean that they are being unsociable: when working with a young horse you need to concentrate on him and his reactions all the time, and any helper or helpers should have enough experience to be able to gauge his reactions. Young horses have short concentration spans (you may be forgiven at times for thinking that they are equivalent to that of a flea) and the trainer's voice and actions must be the only ones they concentrate on.

However, a good trainer will appreciate that at the end of the day, you are the one who is going to carry on his or her work. It should therefore be possible to make appointments to visit your youngster at intervals during the backing process (which will probably last an average of six weeks, depending on how much the horse has done beforehand and how easy or difficult he finds it to adapt to new experiences and surroundings).

During these visiting times, take any opportunity to watch the horse being worked and ask questions afterwards about the methods used. You can carry on the work when you get the horse home and if you want to, perhaps start from scratch with another youngster.

The second approach for someone who has never trained a youngster before is to buy one with an easy going temperament, learn as much as you can in theory and find a friendly expert who is prepared to be at the end of a phone in emergencies (which means asking advice on which way to do something, not expecting them to rush over and sort out your mistakes every time!). There are several good books that will help, notably *Breaking and Schooling* by the same authors and from the same publisher as this book, but obviously books can only offer guidelines.

If you want to buy a youngster specifically to gain experience in breaking and early riding, think about a native pony or one that obviously has a high percentage of native blood. As long as he is up to your weight and has a nice temperament, he will be cheaper to buy and keep, will give you a lot of fun and should be easy to sell on to a nice home if necessary.

Once a horse reaches the age of ten or eleven, his value may start to drop. Here it must be stressed that we are talking about the ordinary horse, for want of a better word: the one who has reached the top of the competition tree and shows every sign of staying there will be a very expensive purchase. Unfortunately some people are reluctant to buy older horses even if a veterinary examination shows that they are perfectly capable of doing the job because they think that from now on things can only go wrong.

In some ways you can understand that line of thinking. We all become less supple as we get older, and the same applies to horses. But if you are buying a horse to have fun with and want one who knows the ropes, an eleven or twelve-year-old horse or even one in his early teens could fit the bill. You have to accept that his value will usually decline as he gets older, so if your circumstances change and you need to find him a home later on you will have to be prepared to take less than you paid for him or even loan him to a suitable home.

Taking on an older horse brings particular responsibilities. If he gives you a lot of fun and has presumably done the same for other people, it is only right to safeguard his interests. Putting him in a sale or taking whatever you can get from a dealer is not on: nothing is worse than going to a sale and seeing old horses catalogued as surplus to requirements. A good dealer will never sell a horse to an unsuitable home because it would reflect badly on their reputation but unless the horse is exceptional, most good dealers would be reluctant to take an animal in its teens even in part exchange against a younger one, simply because they are more difficult to sell.

The unusual thing about buying horses is that few people appreciate that horses may sometimes go down in value. They will happily buy a car and accept that its value will depreciate, and would not expect a washing machine or a television to be worth the same in two years time as when it was bought. But most people insist that a horse must always be worth at least what they paid for it, even if it is no longer as well schooled!

You also have to face the fact that if you take on an older horse, yours might be his last home and the time might come when he can no longer work. This means that he must either be put down or found a useful retirement, which in practice usually means that he will be put down. A horse who has led an active, interesting life is rarely happy if he suddenly gets nothing to do and little attention beyond the minimum care. Sticking an old horse in a field and forgetting about him is passing the buck and not giving him a happy retirement.

Do not let all this doom and gloom put you off the idea of an older horse if there is one that sounds ideal for you. After all, there is no guarantee that a younger horse will stay sound forever: accidents happen, and horses are just as likely as people to fall ill. What you do have to accept is that an older horse, particularly one who has worked hard, will show signs of wear and tear. If you like him, rely on your vet's opinion.

Age tends to be less of a problem in ponies, who tend to live longer and stay sounder. There are plenty of ponies going strong in their twenties and even later—watch any veterans' class at a local show and you will see some very sprightly pensioners!

Sex

Many people profess that they would always choose a gelding as a riding or competition animal in preference to a mare. If you ask them why, they tell you that mares are temperamental and tend to be unpredictable, especially when in season. Whilst some mares may answer this description, there are just as many unpredictable geldings as mares and mares also have their own plus points.

A gelding is, after all, a castrated male: he is not as nature intended him to be. That is not to suggest that we should all start riding stallions: far from it! Most of us have neither the experience or the ability to keep a stallion. But if injury puts an end to a mare's ridden career, then, provided she is good enough, she can hopefully find another job as a brood mare. The key words are if she is good enough: at the very least she must have good conformation, a nice temperament and hopefully she will either have had chance to prove herself or have come from a proven family.

There is an old saying that you tell a gelding, ask a mare and discuss with a stallion. At the risk of making generalisations, geldings tend to be more easy going and less complicated than mares, though there are always exceptions. Riders who get on with mares swear that a good one will always have a head start over a good gelding because she has that extra spark.

Although there have always been good mares in competition, particularly show jumping, they have always been in the minority. They still are, but there are signs that more riders are willing to treat them as individuals. In eventing, for instance, Welton Romance has done well, first for Ginny Elliot and later for Lucy Thompson, whilst Lynn Russell's Wishful Thinking was a successful lightweight and ladies' show hunter who has now gone on to what will hopefully be an equally successful career at stud.

Stallions are also being expected to prove themselves in competition, which can only be a good thing. Jennie Loriston-Clarke showed the way with Dutch Gold, the first of many successful stallions from her Catherston Stud, whilst Endeavour flew the flag in show jumping with Alison Bradley before he was sold to America. In eventing, the Welton stallions from Sam and Linda Barr's Limbury Stud have proved time and time again that talent, temperament and conformation are essential attributes for a stallion.

However, stallions are not for the average rider—nor even for the most experienced ones. Some adapt amazingly well to living in ordinary surroundings, but they must still be treated with respect and must also respect their owners. Thankfully, we have got away from the assumption that stallions are savage beasts who must be kept shut away and beaten into submission when necessary, but whilst the best stallion owners treat their animals with kindness, they know that their natural instincts bring with them the potential for danger.

No matter how experienced you are and how good a temperament a stallion possesses, he will not normally be a feasible proposition unless you can keep him at home in a safe environment and have the time to devote to him. Most livery yards will not be prepared to take a stallion, as they will reckon—usually quite rightly—that it would not be fair on him, their other clients or their horses.

Colour

There is an old saying that a good horse is never a bad colour. Obviously that can be taken two ways but the most sensible interpretation is that if a horse fulfils all your other requirements, it does not really matter what colour he is. However, everyone has likes and dislikes and if you are so set against a particular colour that you would forever be holding it against the horse, you may be better advised to leave him for someone who has no such prejudices and find yourself another.

Many people have a special weakness for coloured horses and ponies.

At the other extreme, there are buyers who look for a horse of a particular colour. This is particularly true of coloured horse, palomino or Appaloosa enthusiasts. Coloured is a term applied in Britain to skewbalds and piebalds, whilst palominos have gold-coloured coats and white manes and tails. Appaloosas, often loosely referred to as spotted horses, have five recognised coat patterns: leopard, blanket, snowflake, frost and marble.

These three have their own societies and their own showing and competition classes, though many can and do compete in open classes against horses of ordinary colour. You may still find show judges who are prejudiced against anything but solid colours; there has yet to be a coloured horse who has won at top level in show hunter classes, though several have done well in workers. Cob judges seem to accept them more readily, and Sue Rawding's beautifully marked grey roan and white Kilkenny Marble, whose darker markings faded as he matured, is a former holder of the Cob of the Year title.

The golden rule if a particular colour is a must is that it should never be allowed to overshadow conformation and temperament. One of the best ways of deciding is to ask yourself whether you would still like the horse if he was plain bay; if the answer is no, because his conformation is not good enough, then the most attractive markings will not compensate for that. Many people find that coloured horses are harder to assess than those of solid colour because their shape is broken up by the different patches. If in doubt, get expert help from an unprejudiced eye.

If you intend to show your horse, it is also important to keep society recommendations in mind. For instance, the perfect coat colour for a palomino is that of a newly minted coin (if you can translate that into real terms!) with no more than three shades leeway either side.

Many traditionalists in the horse world prefer a dark, solid colour: in particular, bay or brown. True black horses are rare and horses that appear to have black coats often have brown hairs and are officially classed as dark brown. They can look wonderful in summer when their coats shine, but some people hate them because they say they are funeral horses.

Greys and chestnuts can also be a case of love it or hate it. A grey may take more work to keep clean, but really stands out in a crowd of dark coloured horses. In showing or dressage, this can be an advantage: after you have seen umpteen boring bays go round, a striking grey makes a welcome change! Chestnuts are often unfairly categorised as being hot-headed, just as redheaded people fall prey to the same pigeon holing. Chestnut mares are an anathema to some horse people, but there are as many chestnut mares who are genuine as there are bay geldings who are not.

Markings have no effect on a horse's ability and very little effect on his hardiness, though horses with white legs may be more prone to mud fever and white feet are said to be softer than dark ones. Some dressage and showing people believe that if a horse has one white sock, it gives the illusion of uneven movement even when the horse is perfectly level and rhythmical. Anyone who believes this is short of excuses or needs glasses.

Vices

Stable vices are the result of the way we keep horses. Wild horses, in the open and grazing most of the time, show no signs of weaving, crib biting or windsucking but it is obviously impossible to keep a domesticated horse in hundreds of acres. Vices which are usually a way of relieving frustration at being restricted to a small space are inevitably the result of modern stable management, though there are cases where grass-kept horses copy a field companion and start cribbing or windsucking on fences.

The three main vices, which under most sale rules must be declared if the horse is offered for sale at auction, are weaving, crib biting and windsucking. They vary in their severity, but basically weaving is when the horse moves from side to side, usually over the stable door; crib biting is when he fixes his teeth on a suitable ledge, usually a door or fence rail and windsucking is when he holds on to a handy surface and gulps in air. Crib biting and windsucking often, though not always, go together.

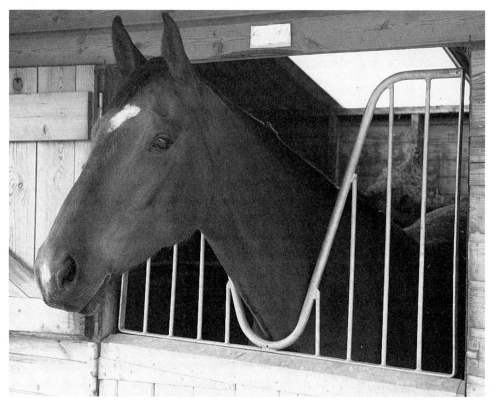

Weaving may present problems if you find you have to sell the horse later on.

Mild weaving, where the horse nods his head from side to side over the door, is perhaps the easiest vice to put up with. Some horses only do it in at feed time in anticipation of a meal; others weave in a way that can affect their soundness, constantly shifting their weight from leg to leg and thus putting strain on their limbs.

In some cases it can be controlled or reduced by clever management—keeping him out as much as possible, making sure he has hay when he is stabled, putting up an anti-weaving grid (a V-shaped metal grid that fixes to the stable door) and so on. Horses who weave in loose boxes usually settle quite happily when kept in stalls, which may seem unacceptable to some owners. However, as long as they are out as much as possible, standing a horse with companions on either side for the times when you need him to be inside cannot be condemned if it leaves him relaxed and happy.

Crib biting puts wear on the horse's teeth and causes damage to stables and fences. There are various foul-tasting products that can be smeared on the horse's favourite cribbing surfaces to discourage him. These can only try to prevent his actions and do not take away the desire to crib, which he will usually do again as soon as he gets the chance.

Crib biters can do a lot of damage to stables and fences.

Windsucking can lead to colic because the horse gulps down air and upsets his digestive system. Not all windsuckers get colic, though some are hard to keep weight on. Other solutions include an operation to make it physically impossible for the horse to arch his neck and get hold of a surface or collars that make it uncomfortable. The traditional anti-cribbing collar has a metal arch that digs into the horse's throat when he attempts to crib and must be removed for him to eat or drink; there is also a new design from America that is said to be more humane and effective.

Other habits that are hard to cope with but are not usually official vices are box walking and rug tearing. A box walker goes round his box like a tiger in a cage, sometimes only when he is excited or worried but in other cases more frequently. Pacing such a small, tight circle obviously adds unwanted strain and these horses make such a mess of their beds that they need more bedding than usual.

Rug tearing is a habit with expensive implications, but can sometimes be cured. A lot of horses have sensitive skins and grab hold of their rugs in their teeth to try to relieve discomfort. Sometimes it is because they are too hot, which can be helped by reducing the number of rugs or using a lighter one, preferably made from breathable fabric.

Alternatively, the rug lining may cause the horse to itch perhaps because it is wool based. Using a rug with a cotton lining or putting a cotton summer sheet under the offending one may solve the problem. If it has become an established habit, sacrificing an old rug and painting it with one of the products designed to stop crib biters can help.

When considering whether or not to buy a horse with a vice, there are several questions to ask yourself. The first one is whether you and anyone else who spends time with him can put up with it. If your horse lives at home and you have to look at him weaving like a top every time you go out the back door, you can soon become wound up and start weaving yourself!

If you intend to keep him on a livery yard, find out whether the owner is prepared to take a horse with a vice. Some will not consider it, for a variety of often good reasons: other owners will worry that their horses will start to copy the offender, whether or not this is likely to happen, and crib biters and windsuckers can do a lot of damage.

Even if none of these considerations causes you any problems, you have to accept that unless the horse is a guaranteed mega star he will be harder to sell than a horse who is free from vice. Never say 'I'm never going to part with him' as circumstances, finances and ambitions can change.

If the horse is exceptionally talented, you may want to follow the philosophy of a leading show jumping trainer: If he does the job, I'm not bothered what he does in his spare time. If he is unlikely to be a star, think twice.

Price

Working out how much a horse is worth is sometimes like asking how long is a piece of string. A leading dealer once said that a horse is worth precisely what someone is prepared to pay for it, which is true enough but not always helpful.

When reading adverts and making inquiries you will find a wide variation in what may seem to be similar horses. This is because some people have an over-inflated idea of their horses' good qualities (or think they can persuade someone else to believe them) whilst some judge their asking price by the state of the market. Others, mainly those from private sellers, may appear remarkably cheap—you may be lucky and find a bargain, but you may also find that the horse has a soundness or behavioural problem.

Auction prices used to be lower than ordinary ones, but this is no longer a general rule. Prestige sales see horses reaching five figures. There are plenty of sales where prices are cheap, but as you will see later, it has to be accepted that there are inherent risks in buying at many of the more run-of-the-mill sales.

Good dealers know exactly what they can expect to get for a horse. Because they are buying and selling all the time, they have a finger on the market pulse: the price you are asked will rarely provide you with a bargain, though it has been known to happen, but should present reasonable value.

Prices for the nice, average all-round horse sometimes vary in different parts of the country, rather like house prices. They tend to follow the same sort of pattern: prices in Scotland will often be lower than those in the densely populated South-East because fewer people are prepared to travel that far. The horse with obvious ability or potential to excel in a particular sphere will always be the exception: many people will travel a long way to look at him and will be prepared to pay a good price.

So can we give any guideline figures? Yes, as long as they are regarded as that and no more. For an ordinary family pony, you are looking at between £350 and £1,000 depending on age, height, conformation, experience and so on. A horse of the same description will perhaps cost between £1,500 and £3,000, with the happy hack at the bottom of the scale and the riding club all-rounder at the top.

Youngsters with potential, whether it is real or fondly imagined, are a wide open market. A weaned foal or yearling may be anything from £600 up to £2,000, a two or unbroken three-year-old from £1,200 up to £3,000. A four-year-old who has been broken and has done his early schooling may be anything from £1,500 up to £4,000 plus.

Horses with a good competition record command appropriate prices. If we use our £3,000 riding club all-rounder as a baseline—by that we mean a horse that can do a nice novice dressage test and jump a three foot three to three foot six course—you can build on that until you get to the £5,000 to £7,000 range for an animal with BSJA winnings or horse trials or dressage points.

Looking for a Badminton star or a potential Olympic dressage horse or show jumper? Then you either need a good eye and a lot of luck or a bank balance that can absorb telephone number prices. But whatever you are searching for, remember that there are so many variables it is impossible to set hard and fast price rules.

In the end, it is what the horse is worth to you as a buyer that is important, though you and the seller must be on common ground before you start. It is no good telling the owner of a Grade B show jumper advertised at £10,000 that he is only worth £2,500 to you!

Chapter 6
Different Ways of Buying a Horse

There are four ways of buying a horse: from a private seller, from a dealer, through an agent or agency, and at an auction. All have advantages and disadvantages from the buyer's point of view, but there is no hard and fast rule that makes one avenue better than another. It depends on your experience, the time and money you have available and whether or not luck is on your side!

If a horse is for sale, there must be a reason. Most reasons are perfectly acceptable: for instance, the owner wants something with more ability, or their circumstances have changed. Horses are often advertised because an owner has become pregnant, or is about to go to college or university, or cannot reconcile the demands of a job with the demands of keeping a horse. Equally, a dealer sells horses as a way of making a living and studs breed horses to sell, not to collect.

Anyone selling a horse will want to present it in the best possible light and if they are looking for a buyer because they do not get on with the horse and cannot stand the sight of it any longer, they are hardly likely to tell you. It is not that people selling horses are any less honest than people selling anything else; after all, if you put your house on the market you emphasise its good points, not its bad ones. The fact remains, though, that however desperate you are to find the right horse and however nice the seller seems, you must let your head rule your heart.

The Latin warning, *Caveat emptor* (Let the buyer beware) should be engraved on the heart and the cheque book of anyone buying a horse. It would be foolish and wrong to assume that all sellers will tell you lies, or at least be economical with the truth, but never allow enthusiasm to sweep away common sense.

Litigation resulting from the buying and selling of horses has become increasingly common over the past few years. Most of this stems from the fact that many of today's riders do not have a horsey background and assume that buying a horse is the same as buying a car or a washing machine. Perhaps life would be simpler if it were, but until someone invents the mechanical horse, it never will be.

Horses are living beings with minds of their own. There is no guarantee an animal that performs beautifully for one rider will do the same for anyone: it is up to the buyer to be as sure as possible that he can get the same tune out of the horse as the seller, and it is up to the seller to represent the animal as fairly as possible. At one time, if you bought a horse and the relationship failed to click, you either persevered until things improved or sold it to someone who was more likely than you to get on with it.

Nowadays buyers are perhaps too ready to buy in a hurry and start ringing their solicitors if things do not go according to plan. Whilst no one would want buyers or sellers to lack the protection of consumer law, and it is essential that they are able to turn to it when all else fails, it is a fact of life that horses and consumer legislation do not always go together precisely because horses are not cars or washing machines.

The legal perspective

So what sort of protection do you have in law? Basically, everyone is covered by common law, which encompasses issues such as the duty of care and negligence and the Misrepresentation Act 1967. The Sale of Goods Act is more complicated. One section of this Act defines a contract of sale of goods as a contract by which the seller agrees to transfer the property in goods to the buyer for a money consideration called the price. The Act applies to everyone who comes within this definition, but other sections relating to merchantable quality and fitness for purpose relate only to the seller acting in the course of a business.

The next question, inevitably, is: so when is a dealer not a dealer? We all know about the private sellers who move house or are pregnant three times a year, but there is no clear definition of a dealer. So far, the only guideline is the one from the Inland Revenue that a dealer is someone who sells six or seven items of the same or similar nature a year.

This is sometimes used as the starting point in any legal action where the point has to be determined. Similarly, some newspapers and magazines print a statement that anyone selling a certain number of horses per year—the figure ranges from three upwards—is not considered to be a private seller. Anyone placing an advertisement under such guidelines would probably be considered to accept the terms.

If a horse is bought at auction or through an agent, this is a different situation again. Auctions have their own conditions of sale, which should be stated in the catalogue, though these do not affect your basic rights. However, they do not give the full protection of the Sale of Goods Act unless the auction terms are so stringent that they amount to the same thing.

One of the main considerations with agency sales is whether negotiations are entered into between buyer and agent, or whether the agent merely introduces the buyer to the seller. This can affect negotiations where, for instance, a dealer sells a horse on behalf of its owner instead of buying the animal from the owner and selling it on again.

For instance, X is a dealer who, through a friend of a friend, knows Y. Y wants to sell her horse and X says that she will advertise it for her. X, who has never seen the horse, asks Y for a description of the animal; X then advertises the horse with Y's phone number so that Y and the potential buyer, Z, can negotiate direct.

X then charges a small fee to cover the cost of the advertisement and her expertise in wording it. If things go wrong after the purchase and there is any legal recourse by Z, the likely liability would fall with Y, not X.

It could be different if X advertises the horse, informs Z that she is selling it on behalf of Y and negotiates the sale on Y's behalf in return for a commission. Z could then have possible legal recourse against both X as the agent and Y as the principal.

Before you console yourself that if you did want or need to take legal action, you would just simply find a good solicitor, think again. Getting the right legal advice about horse purchase problems can be easier said than done. It is vital that the legal expert used should be conversant with consumer law and also understands horses; finding someone with both skills is difficult, though some firms are now advertising specialist skills in equestrian litigation. Whether this is a good thing or an unfortunate sign of the times is open to debate!

Buying privately

Many buyers assume that buying a horse from a private seller—in other words, someone who is not a professional dealer—will mean paying a smaller price and running less risk of being taken for a ride. If you take into account the cost of making a mistake, neither of these suppositions hold water.

Some private sellers are knowledgeable, sensible people who know exactly what their horse is and is not. They know what sort of home and job would suit him and have studied the current market so they know how to set a reasonable price. These sorts of people are a joy to do business with.

Others are, to put it bluntly, a real pain. You can find sellers who have a vastly optimistic view of their horse's conformation, ability and even height and seem to have plucked a large figure out of thin air when setting a price. Sometimes they read other advertisements, decide that one sounds rather like their horse and that their animal must therefore be worth the same: the fact that the other horse is better looking, better schooled and has more ability is besides the point!

Another common problem is the private seller who paid £X thousand for a horse and assumes that he has a divine right to make a profit. The fact that the horse was well-schooled with recent competition winnings when they bought it, and now goes less well and is less successful, is something they choose to ignore. Horses can lose their value as quickly as a good rider can increase their value, and once a horse reaches his peak he is not going to command ever higher prices.

This is not meant to be a damning indictment of private sellers, just as the next sections are not meant to be condemnations of dealers, auctions or agents. It is, however, an indication that you have to be able to analyse the judgement of every seller and with some private ones, your judgement may be even more crucial if you are to avoid wasting time, money and temper.

Buying from a dealer

Everyone knows horror stories about shady dealers, and some of them are undoubtedly true. But by picking the right dealer and using a good horse vet to examine your potential purchase, the chance of buying the right horse this way is as good as any other. The first step in finding the right dealer is to ensure that they are just that: there are far too many people who turn over the odd horse or three, or four every few months and insist that they are private sellers.

You can spot them by the phone numbers that appear with depressing regularity at the end of advertisements, accompanied by claims such as the aforesaid 'owner pregnant' or 'sale due to house move' every couple of months. 'Owner overstocked' is sometimes another favourite.

A reputable dealer will be happy to be known as such; it is, after all, his living and making a living depends on building up and keeping a good reputation. There is a world of difference between the pretend dealer who buys a horse cheaply because it has a problem, sells it on for a few pounds and disappears into the woodwork and the dealer who has a constant supply of correctly assessed and described animals. The former is thinking only of the immediate sale and never mind the consequences, whereas the latter is looking ahead to future business.

After all, if you buy a horse from Joe Bloggs and it turns out to be a dud, you are hardly going to recommend him to your friends when they are looking for horses. But if Joe Bloggs uses his skills and contacts to find you a horse that suits you, your friends will be so impressed by the way you and your new horse get on together that they will ask him to do the same for them. Successful dealers make their living through repeat business by recommendation from one client to another, and by satisfied clients returning when they want another horse.

It is not in a dealer's interests to sell you an unsuitable horse, as they are liable under the Sale of Goods Act to sell goods (i.e., horses) that are of merchantable quality and fit for the purpose for which they are sold. He will be well aware of this, and will also be used to summing up riders' abilities and ambitions (and working out the difference between the real and the imagined). If you describe the sort of horse you would like to own, and he realises when you meet him and try various animals that your dream horse is not actually the one that would best suit you, he will try and persuade you to shift your perspective towards the latter.

A dealer who specialises in the sort of horse you are looking for may be a good source. Lynn Russell competed successfully on this show cob before selling him to an amateur owner/rider who did equally well.

It is all very well getting you to part with a large sum of money for a top class competition animal, but if he knows that you lack the experience to make the most of its ability or even that you could run into trouble with it he will not want you telling everyone that you bought it from him. If he can persuade you towards the all-round riding club horse that he knows would be much more suitable, and you will have fun and success with, he will enhance both your reputations.

Some dealers specialise in the sort of horses they compete on themselves, such as show jumpers or show horses. A few people are reluctant to buy from them because they think that if the animal was any good, the dealer would keep it for himself. This logic is flawed and will often lose them the chance of a good buy.

A dealer who specialises in, for example, show horses will have a wide range of contacts who know that he will always be in the market for a good horse. He will also know exactly what the judges look for and whether an animal has what it takes. Most important of all, he will be able to spot potential in the rough and match up rider to horse. Looking at a muddy overgrown pony with a mane down to its knees and feathers on its heels and realising that it could be a winning show cob takes years of experience and a natural eye that some people never achieve.

Such a dealer will only be satisfied with the very best for himself. He wants the horse that will win Wembley, not the one that will get consistent placings at a lower level. Naturally everyone who is interested in showing dreams of cantering under the Wembley spotlight, just as everyone who enjoys novice eventing dreams of winning Badminton—but how many can realistically hope to be in with a chance? And when it comes down to it, how many riders get just as much pleasure from winning at the level at which they are happy?

Because such a dealer is always looking for the potential top horse, lots will pass through his hands that will not reach the giddy heights but will give a lot of pleasure and satisfaction. Go back to our basics and be realistic, and this could be your answer.

Although dealers may be reluctant to admit it, they do occasionally make mistakes. It is not unknown for a potential star to slip through the net, perhaps because the horse needed the one-to-one attention that a private owner enjoys but which is hard to achieve on a busy yard. No one is infallible!

You will be unlikely to get a bargain from a dealer, but you should get a nice horse at a realistic price. Another advantage is that you will often be able to see more than one horse at the same time, which might not sound important before you start looking, but may well seem attractive if you drive a long way to see one horse that turns out to be unsuitable. Another plus point in buying from a dealer is that if despite all the efforts on both sides, you do not get on with the horse or if you later want to move on to something with more ability most dealers will take the horse back in part exchange. Such a transaction will inevitably involve you parting with more money, but for some people that is a price worth paying to avoid the hassle of selling a horse privately.

Some dealers take horses to sell on behalf of their owners. This does not necessarily mean that there is something wrong with the horse, and, if there is, the dealer should have the skill to spot it, sort it out or return the horse to its owner. Many private sellers do not have the time or inclination to deal with a stream of potential purchasers, or the facilities to show off the horse to its best advantage, and sending it to be sold on their behalf is a good solution. It also means that the horse stands an excellent chance of being matched up with the right rider, so he benefits as well.

Buying through an agency

Over the past few years agencies have become more common. Specialist bloodstock agencies, who concentrate on Thoroughbreds for the racing market, have been part of that world for a long time but are not usually looking at the same market as the average non-racing buyer. There are many other specialist agencies ranging from ones for coloured horse enthusiasts to those aiming to bring together buyers and sellers of dressage or event horses.

Agencies vary in the approach they take. Some are simply another way of offering advertisements: sellers supply details of their horses and the agencies send them out to potential purchasers. They usually rely on the sellers for the accuracy of the description provided and will not be held responsible for any inaccuracies; so if you travel to see a 16hh event horse that turns out to be 15.2hh, the answer is the same as if the scenario had occurred with a private seller—hard luck!

Reputable agencies do impress upon their clients how important it is to be accurate in their descriptions. After all, if a potential buyer feels that his time has been wasted looking at one horse, he might decide it is not worth bothering with any other on the agency list and the agency loses out.

A few agencies go out and see every horse before it is put on their books. They, rather than the owners, supply the descriptions so as long as the person responsible is knowledgeable, you may sometimes get a truer picture. A minority take the procedure even farther and take videos of the horses to show to potential customers. If the videos are of a good standard, this can be particularly useful; you ought to be able to get a good impression of the horse's overall conformation, movement and jumping style.

However the agency is run, the golden rule should be that it charges sellers but never buyers. If you are asked to pay a charge to register or to have details of horses sent to you, it cannot be recommended that you deal with this particular concern. The only charge that is understandable is if you are asked to pay a returnable deposit on a video.

When horses are taken into a yard to be produced and sold on, the line between dealer and agency may cross over. A good dealer will always make it clear whether the horse belongs to him, or whether he is selling it on behalf of a client. If in doubt, ask.

Buying at an auction

In the bloodstock world, buying and selling at auction has always been the accepted way of doing business and no one thinks twice about it. The Continentals have a similar attitude: Paul Shockemohle's Performance Sales International attracts many overseas buyers for potential jumping horses, where sales figures run into hundreds of thousands, and the Verdun sales of elite German dressage horses and potential dressage stars have a similarly wide catchment area. In Britain, we are slowly realising that sales are not always a hotbed of dishonesty and iniquity: up-market events have fought an uphill, but now seemingly successful, battle to match buyers and sellers this way.

Sales for racehorses in and out of training, such as those at Ascot, attract many non-racing buyers and are often a good place for an experienced rider to find a Thoroughbred that can be re-routed to another job. Finally, there are perhaps the least glamorous sales of all—those held at cattle market type venues.

In different ways, none of these kinds of auction is a place for a novice buyer. The prestige sales tend to offer horses with talent or potential that could only be exploited by expert riders; the horses have often been kept at the venue for a few weeks prior to sale and schooled by expert riders, and a youngster may well need letting down for a period so it can settle into a new home and start work. Buying from a racehorse sale inevitably means taking home a fit Thoroughbred that knows no existence other than racing and all the associated problems that brings. Again, these horses need letting down before they can be re-schooled and re-schooling a racehorse is not for a novice.

Both the racehorse and cattle market type sales have no trial facilities (not that you could get on a racehorse and try it as if it was an ordinary riding horse) so it takes a lot of skill and luck to make a successful purchase. It may well be a case of buying a horse with your fingers crossed, taking it home and then finding out just what you have paid for. If the result is not what you hoped for, you have not only the horse's keep to pay for in the interim but also the task of selling him again.

One of the essentials for anyone buying a horse is to learn how to read a sales catalogue and, just as important, how to read between the lines. Start at the terms and conditions of sale, which run along broad parallel lines but are not always the same.

All auctions have warranties that may be applied to horses offered for sale. There is also a time limit on how long these apply; you often have no more than 48 hours in which to find out if there is anything wrong and inform the auctioneers so that the horse can be returned.

The most important factor is whether or not the horse is warranted sound but the definition of this is not always the same. Some sales define warranted sound as being sound in wind, eyes, heart and action whereas others restrict it to wind, eyes and action only; under the second qualification, a horse could legitimately be sold as sound even if the owner knew it could drop dead the next day because of a faulty heart.

Prestige sales, where horses have to undergo a full pre-purchase veterinary examination at the sale before the transaction is concluded, give the greatest protection on soundness. Some sales insist that a similar examination, including X-rays of the front feet, is carried out before the horse is accepted for sale. Other auctions offer buyers the chance to have the horse vetted by one of a team of vets at the actual sale, but these examinations vary in scope. Some may consist of no more than trotting the horse up to see if it looks sound, examining its eyes and listening to its heart and lungs. Sales where a vetting procedure is offered often describe the horses coming under the hammer as sold subject to re-examination.

You need to pay great attention to the wording in the catalogue. This applies to everything, but to soundness in particular. If the catalogue entry describes the horse as believed sound and it turns out not to be when you get it home, you have absolutely no comeback. Believed sound is the seller's opinion; if it is a wrong one, the only loser is the buyer.

You cannot assume that a horse is not sound because he is not warranted as such;

there may be occasions when a seller wants to be sure that he takes a horse to a sale and does not bring it back again, and is not prepared to risk it being returned. However, it takes a brave or foolhardy purchaser (take your pick as to which applies) to bid for a horse knowing it may have a problem.

Many sales state that details of age, height and breeding as carried in the catalogues are not warranties. That does not usually matter much as far as height is concerned since your eye should tell you whether the horse meets your requirements or not. But if height is particularly important, perhaps because you are buying a horse to show in a class where height limits are imposed, you cannot complain if you get your 15.1hh bargain show cob home and he turns out to be 15.1hh and half an inch.

Age is obviously more of a worry. If a horse has documentation to prove its age, perhaps a Thoroughbred passport, it should be available for inspection and you will be able to check that papers and horse actually match. But if a horse described as a seven-year-old actually turns out to be nearer seventeen, you may find yourself without any comeback.

Most sales state that some stable vices, usually crib biting, windsucking and weaving, must be declared. Box walking, where the horse walks round and round his box like a tiger in a cage, can take a heavy toll on the horse's limbs and condition and means you will use twice as much bedding. It may not be stipulated as a vice that needs declaring. In that case, you are stuck with it. You also have to remember the time limit on returns: if a horse is so busy looking at his new surroundings for the first three days that he forgets to weave, you have no comeback under a 48-hour rule if he starts again on the fourth!

Always remember that catalogue descriptions, like advertisements, may range from the totally truthful to the totally fanciful. Look for statements of fact, not opinions. Even then, you have to be careful; most sales have definitions that are applied to various descriptions, but these too can be open to interpretation. For instance, the sale conditions may state that a horse or pony described as quiet to ride must be good in traffic and quiet to ride in all paces, which sounds comforting. But one person's definition of quiet to ride may not be another's, so beware.

A horse described in a particular way must be capable of doing that job. For instance, a show jumper must be capable of jumping a course of show jumps but the description could apply whether they were two feet or five feet high. Similarly, a hunter must be capable of being hunted, but you cannot complain if you want to go jumping across trappy country and he has been used on Exmoor with never a fence in sight.

One of the funniest definitions applies to movement. It is no good buying a horse described as a good mover and complaining because a more knowledgeable person points out that it dishes or brushes. In auction terms, a good mover only means that the horse is not lame!

When buying a horse privately or from a dealer, you have the chance to ride it in different surroundings, such as in a schooling area, in the open and on the roads. When buying a horse at auction you may have the chance to ride it in an enclosed area and over a few show jumps, but you will not be able to ride it in the open and will certainly not be allowed to hack it out on the roads. This means that you need to read the catalogue descriptions carefully and be aware that there are many ways of interpreting things.

A horse who is described as not a novice ride may be more than you bargained for.

For instance, a horse described as 'not a novice ride' could be anything from a responsive, sensitive animal who only goes well for a rider with good balance and light hands to a total headcase who is likely to buck, rear or tank off with you as soon as you settle in the saddle. Likewise, a 'strong ride' or 'suitable for a man' could be a powerful, onward bound horse or he could be a tearaway who tries to set off at full gallop as soon as his feet touch grass.

Look at what is and what is not said. A horse might be good to box, clip, catch and shoe but that does not mean it is good in traffic. Similarly, an unbroken four-year-old might have been left to mature, but as most would at least have been backed by then, it might be such a hooligan that the owner has decided to let someone else risk their neck trying to do the job.

Most auctions are places for people with plenty of experience of buying horses. If you are keen to make a purchase this way and do not fit the description, either find someone who does and ask him or her to act as your adviser or be prepared to take pot luck. It has to be said that auctioneers want buyers and sellers to be happy with a transaction, and many auctioneers will do everything possible to help—but it is not their job to baby-sit naïve bargain hunters.

When you hear of a suitable sale, send off for a catalogue and go through it carefully. Start by reading the terms and conditions and then find all the likely sounding horses who are catalogued with the warranties you have decided are essential. Do not get carried away by descriptions of horses that sound lovely but are not actually what you are looking for: that four-year-old Thoroughbred mare thought certain to make a top class event horse will not suit you if you are looking for an experienced cob to hack and generally enjoy. In any case, 'thought likely to make' a top class anything is a description that holds no real value. It might be just as described, or you might watch it go through the ring and find that it is a nervy, weedy type with curby hocks and weak quarters.

Some entries may be available for inspection and vetting prior to the auction; this is usually phrased as 'may be seen and tried prior to sale by appointment with the auctioneer.' The reason arrangements are made through the auctioneer is that they will still expect the horse to go through the sales ring; if all the good horses sell beforehand there are fewer attractions for potential buyers. Occasionally horses are sold beforehand, but the buyer is still supposed to notify the auctioneer (who has acted as an agent) and pay the commission.

If a horse sounds really interesting it is worth going to see it beforehand, as you will have more time to inspect it and should be able to try it in different surroundings, such as on the roads. Even when sales boast trials facilities, you will be limited to an indoor or outdoor arena.

The sale catalogue will indicate at what time horses are to be sold and what payment arrangements will be accepted. Unless you are known to the auctioneers as a regular buyer and have made arrangements with them, this usually means cash or a banker's draft. If you do not want to risk carrying a large wad of banknotes around, then make arrangements with your bank so that the auctioneers know you are guaranteed to make a payment up to a certain sum.

Arrive at the sale as early as possible to give plenty of time to view the possibles you have marked. You will be able to look at the horses in their stables or lines (depending on the sale set-up) and will also be able to see them trotted up: follow the guidelines in Chapter 8.

If the person with the horse is its owner, you can ask any questions not covered by the catalogue description; for example, is it good in traffic, does it load well, etc? How much credence you place on the answer depends on your faith in and your ability to read human nature. You may find that the person with the horse is not its owner (or does not want to admit to being such) and may even profess to know nothing about it. You makes your bid and you takes your chance!

If there is a trial area, watch the horse being ridden and see how it goes for its owner or its representative. Watch, too, how they show it off. Is it ridden equally on both reins or do they stick to one, probably the one on which it goes best but perhaps the one on which a slight lameness does not show? If there is a jump, do they show what it is like over a fence even if it is just a small cross pole? What are the horse's reactions to others around it: does it work reasonably calmly, or does it lay its ears back every time another horse comes anywhere near?

Watch how it goes for anyone else who tries it and ask if you may ride it. Most vendors will be happy to allow this, but be cautious of anyone who refuses. They may feel, often rightly, that their horse could be upset being ridden by lots of unknown riders; equally, they may be worried that, given the chance, it will stage a rodeo display or attempt the fastest lap time of the trial area!

Be very careful about horses who arrive late. There may be a genuine reason, but it may also be that the vendor hopes to sell on first impressions rather than giving people time to work out what his horse's problems are!

If you decide to bid for a horse, set yourself a limit and stick to it. It is too easy to get carried away in the heat of the moment and go over your limit, when perhaps you would not have dreamed of doing so if you were buying in more ordinary circumstances. Remember that horses are sold in guineas; a guinea is a pound and five pence, so if you bid one thousand guineas you are due to pay one thousand, one hundred pounds. This is not just a quaint old-fashioned custom or a clever way of parting you from more money than you realised: usually the pounds go to the seller and the pence represent the auctioneer's commission.

Stand where you can attract the auctioneer's attention as the horse you are interested in comes into the ring. The auctioneer will ask for a starting price, which may or may not be close to what he eventually hopes to get, and will take a lower one to get the wheels rolling. If you want to enter the bidding, hold your catalogue in your hand and raise it to attract his attention.

Once he knows you are in the negotiations, he will keep an eye on you and do his best to encourage other bidders to go higher. If the horse has been entered with a reserve price, which means that the seller has told the auctioneer that it must not be sold for less than a certain sum, he cannot take a lower bid even if it is that last one. It is then up to you to find out the reserve from the auctioneer's office or from the vendor and decide whether you want to pay that.

If you buy a horse outside the ring and the sale is booked through the auctioneer, you have the protection of any warranties stated in the category. If you come to a private arrangement with the vendor, which is against the terms of the sale but is not unknown, you have absolutely no comeback at all if things go wrong. For instance, if the horse is sold sound and turns out not to be, you would be covered by the terms and conditions of the sale if sale arrangements were made at the sale, through the auctioneer but if you leave him out of it, you are stuck with any problems. Some vendors may try and persuade you to do a private deal because in theory they do not then have to pay the auctioneer's commission, but it is not a straight way of doing things.

If the horse is sold without reserve, or the reserve is reached, the auctioneer will often indicate this. As soon as it becomes clear that the bidding ceiling has been reached and no one is going to make any further bids, he will announce 'Sold' and bring down his hammer. If yours is the successful bid, the horse becomes your property as soon as that happens—subject to a veterinary examination if he is sold sound and under those conditions. It is no good changing your mind because you suddenly realise that he has a curb that you did not spot earlier, or because you got carried away and bid more than you really wanted to pay.

Chapter 7
Sharing, Loaning and Yards

Most people choose to buy a horse because they feel that they are then beholden to only their own sense of responsibility. Others prefer to share the use of a horse with his owner, or take one on loan. There may be circumstances where this is a good course to pursue, but loan or share arrangements do not necessarily provide an easy option.

Any arrangement must be entered into in a businesslike way, even if it is between yourself and a friend. Relying on vague conversations and assumptions is a quick route to irritation, spoilt friendships and even heartbreak.

There are lots of good reasons why people want to share or loan their horse. Perhaps a working owner does not have the time to look after and ride the horse but cannot afford to pay for full livery, or the owners of an outgrown pony do not want to sell him because a younger child will be ready to ride him in a couple of years.

Sharing

Sharing usually means that the ownership of the horse stays with the original person and you are asked to help with the cost of his keep and perhaps the work involved in looking after him in exchange for sharing the riding. Be very wary about buying a share in a horse, as this can lead to all sorts of problems: what happens if you disagree over his use, or one of you decides you want to sell your share?

Just as you would not buy a horse you did not feel happy riding, so you must be careful when looking for one to share. It goes without saying that the owner will be even more careful about you: be prepared to be put under scrutiny and subjected to cross examination. Also ensure that you and the horse's owner can get on and form a partnership; there has to be a certain amount of give and take on both sides, but the final responsibility and authority will rest with the owner.

In some ways, sharing a horse can be a good introduction to owning one. It gives you a taste of the responsibility and commitment involved, but hopefully it also means that you have back-up and guidance. The drawbacks are that someone else is always in control and you may not be able to ride whenever it suits you, or perhaps compete.

You may find advertisements from people wanting to share their horse in magazines, the horses for sale column in your local newspaper or on noticeboards in tack shops and feed merchants. Before trying a horse, find out exactly what sort of arrangement the owner wants and decide if you would be happy with it.

Many working owners look for sharers who can ride during the week, but want the full use of their horses at weekends. This may suit someone who is at home with a family and can spare time on weekdays, but you may feel you need an arrangement where you can ride on at least one day during the weekend.

If you are being asked to help look after the horse, can you juggle your commitments to suit his routine? On the financial side, is the owner looking to split all costs—including things like insurance premiums—straight down the middle, or just the basic ones?

The best share arrangements seem to be those where only one partner wants to compete, or when partners are interested in different disciplines, for example, dressage and show jumping. Most owners will be happy for you to have lessons on the horse, but may stipulate that it must be with the same person who teaches them so that you are both working to the same guidelines.

Ask the same sort of questions about the horse as if you were buying him (see Chapter 8.) The advantage here is that as the owner is not trying to get rid of the horse, they are much more likely to be forthcoming about any problems! If the horse is not totally reliable in traffic, or tends to be excitable, do not feel guilty about admitting that you feel he would be more than you could handle. Be honest about your own experience and ability, and if an exploratory phone call sounds promising, arrange to meet up with the owner and horse.

If you like the horse, it is a good idea to ask the owner to ride him for you. This enables you to see not only how the horse goes, but also how the owner rides; in some ways the two go together, but you will at least get an impression of whether he is forward going or on the lazy side, well-schooled or otherwise.

Unless you think you could not possibly manage him, ask if you can have a ride. Try not to be too nervous or self-conscious about the owner watching you; remember it might have been just as nerve-racking for her. Just think about the horse and get the feel of him.

He has to get used to you just as much as you have to get used to him, so be tactful and ask for a little at a time. Follow a similar pattern to that suggested in the next chapter, as if you were actually buying him: work on both reins, carry out some upwards and downwards transitions and ride some circles, serpentines and so on.

If you intend to jump him and the work on the flat goes well, begin with a small cross pole at trot and build up until you are cantering to an upright fence. The height does not matter: you can tell whether you are going to establish balance and rhythm just as easily over two foot six as over four feet.

It should not take long for you (and the horse's owner) to work out if you all stand a good chance of getting on. If the signs are promising, ask if you can go for a short hack with someone. Perhaps the horse's owner can borrow a mount from another owner on the yard, or persuade them to go out with you.

Again, be modest in your ambitions. A short hack that enables you to meet traffic, trot and perhaps canter if the going and terrain permit, will show you if you are going to enjoy the horse. If you intend to or have to hack out on your own sometimes, check that the horse is used to this and that the owner is happy for you to do so.

Hopefully you will feel that things could work out, but if you have any doubts, be honest. Try not to be offended if the horse's owner does not feel that you are the right sort of rider, particularly if you are fairly inexperienced. This one might not work out, but eventually you will find one that will.

If all goes well, work out a written agreement with the horse's owner. It is the only way to ensure that you each understand what the other expects, and also spells out who pays for what, and when. If your arrangement involves looking after the horse at times, you will have to spend time with the owner learning the routine she follows—the horse will be happiest if you stick to it, and you will avoid small but irritating niggles such as how much fresh bedding is put down.

Many sharers start off with a trial period, then work on a theoretical notice period if one partner wants to back out. Unless you have an almighty row, which means you never want to see each other again, this is the fairest system.

Loaning

Taking a horse or pony on loan usually means you are solely responsible for his care and running costs. Again, it is important to have a written agreement, particularly if it is a loan with a view to purchase arrangement.

Some owners want to sell their animals but are anxious to do all they can to find the right homes. A loan period of, say, six months may therefore be suggested if you like the horse and his owner thinks you would be suitable for each other. It will often be stipulated that the horse stays at his present yard during the loan period, which is fair enough: if things do not work out, he has not suffered too much disruption and his owner can pick up the reins again. It is important with this sort of arrangement that an eventual purchase price is agreed at the beginning. It must also be agreed that the sale's completion is subject to a successful pre-purchase veterinary examination (see Chapter 9).

Loaning involves a certain amount of risk, as does buying. If it is a straightforward loan rather than a loan with a view to purchase, the owner may change her mind four months later and say she wants to sell the horse. You then have to decide if you can afford to or want to buy him, or if you are going to walk away from the arrangement.

It has also been known for owners to loan out horses that have behavioural problems or are in poor condition, wait for the person who takes them to sort them out and then announce that they are going to sell them. In theory a written agreement could contain a clause guaranteeing you compensation or commission if this happened, but in practice you would have to go through the hassle and uncertainty of legal action with no guaranteed result.

Your loan agreement should cover every aspect of the horse's management. You may wish to ask a solicitor to either draw one up or check your suggested version; in all fairness, you can only expect a solicitor to cover every point if they have equestrian knowledge. The following agreement, which could be adapted for sharers and must be signed and dated by both parties, may give you some ideas but it is only a guideline.

Loan agreement entered into on (date) between (name and address) hereafter known as the owner and (name and address) hereafter known as the borrower.

This agreement relates to the 16hh eight-year-old bay Thoroughbred cross Welsh Cob mare known as Meg. This horse will remain the property of (owner's name and address).

The agreed loan period is for (duration) beginning on (date) and can be terminated by either party on one/two months' written notice (as appropriate). The owner has the right to remove Meg without notice if not satisfied that she is being kept according to the conditions of this agreement.

Meg is to be kept at (address of stables) and the owner's permission must be given before she is moved.

The owner is responsible for insuring Meg and for veterinary costs arising out of illness or accident, excluding vaccination, dental care and worming costs. The borrower is responsible for all feeding, stabling, grazing and farrier's costs and also for vaccination, worming and dental care costs.

The borrower agrees that Meg is attended by the farrier at intervals no greater than every six weeks and that organisation of this and other day to day care are his/her responsibility.

The borrower agrees that the owner be notified of any illness or injury as soon as possible and that a veterinary surgeon be called out whenever necessary. If the owner cannot be contacted, the borrower has the authority to act on a veterinary surgeon's instructions.

Meg may be used for activities specified in the owner's insurance policy (details) but must not be used for any outside this.

The owner reserves the right to visit Meg once a month and to give 24 hours' notice of the visit when possible.

Another way of loaning a horse is to apply to one of the schemes run by established horse charities, notably the International League for the Protection of Horses. The ILPH, which has its headquarters in Norfolk and also has British centres in Aberdeenshire and Surrey, is a worldwide organisation dedicated to the welfare of all equines.

Animals that are given over to the ILPH are assessed, rested and rehabilitated when necessary and re-homed to suitable borrowers. It must be emphasised that this is not just a cheap way of getting a horse: the conditions are stringent, there is a waiting list of would-be borrowers and you have to be prepared to make just as much commitment as if you were buying a horse, perhaps even more so.

Horses and ponies come to the ILPH for all sorts of reasons. Some are left to it in their owners' wills so that the owners know that they will have a guaranteed future: ILPH horses are never sold. Others are victims of cruelty, or may have behavioural problems that their owners cannot cope with. The skill of the ILPH's staff is so great that many horses previously thought of as lost causes have been rehabilitated and found homes where they lead successful, useful and settled lives.

The animals that go there range from ponies to potential competition horses, so whether you hope to find a happy hack or an animal with competition potential, the chances are that the ILPH will eventually be able to match you with a suitable partner. This assumes, of course, that you match its requirements: anyone who applies to join the loan scheme has to pass strict criteria.

The first step is to join the ILPH if you are not already a member—something everyone who cares about horses should think about. You then fill in a loan application form, available by sending a stamped addressed envelope to the ILPH at Anne Colvin House, Snetterton, Norfolk NR16 2LR.

The premises where you intend to keep the animal will be inspected by one of its field officers, all former mounted police officers who are as good at dealing with people as they are with horses. If all goes well, your application will go on file and you will be invited to see and try a likely sounding animal when one is ready to be put out on loan. Hopefully both you and the ILPH assessor will think there is a good chance that you will strike up a partnership and after signing a formal agreement you will be able to take the horse home.

Part of the agreement stipulates that you must be prepared to accept spot check visits by a field officer at any time. This and other formalities are not as terrifying as they may sound; everything is done on a friendly but thorough basis because the animal's welfare has to come first.

Finding a livery yard

The final step before looking for your dream horse is to ensure that you have somewhere suitable to keep him. If you are lucky enough to have your own land and stables this is one problem you do not have to worry about, but most people have to keep their horses in rented accommodation and perhaps in some sort of livery system.

If you are buying a horse to replace another one and are happy with your present yard, you should not have any problems. Be prepared to pay at least a retainer on the facilities you rent, as the yard owner could probably replace you rather more easily than you could find another yard. Most yards will charge the basic rent of stable and grazing, but if the horse has been kept on full livery and the owner has a waiting list of prospective clients, you may be asked to pay more.

Is an outdoor school essential for your training programme?

If you want to jump, are the facilities adequate?

There are two ways of looking at this. From your point of view, you obviously do not want to pay for feed, bedding and care that your horse is not getting but remember that the yard owner still has to pay wages, maintenance costs and so on. If there is a waiting list of people wanting to bring horses to the yard, every week you are without a horse is in effect costing the yard owner money. In the end, it comes down to how much you value the yard, how much the yard owner values you and whether or not it would be easy to find a set-up that suits you as well.

If you have sold a horse and are looking for a more high-powered replacement, perhaps so that you can compete regularly or at a higher level, does your current yard offer the facilities you will need? You do not need to think in terms of Olympic-sized dressage arenas and full cross-country and show jumping courses, but you will need a schooling area that offers year round good going. If you intend to fit in your riding around home and work commitments—and that applies to most of us—do you need an indoor school or floodlit outdoor one so you can work your horse on dark winter mornings and/or evenings?

If you are looking for a yard for the first time, be prepared to put time, thought and even money into the search. A lot of people will tell you that it will take you so long to find a horse that you do not need to worry about finding him somewhere to live until the deal is nearly completed, but if you follow this philosophy you are taking a big risk.

Even if you find your ideal yard straight away, you cannot guarantee that there will be a vacancy. And though it may not happen very often, it has been known for the very first horse you look at to be the ideal one. The better your initial research, the more likely this is to happen, simply because you will have weeded out many unsuitable animals without actually going to look at them.

When you consider how much you are going to put into your new horse, in terms of time and ambition as well as money, it can be a good investment to pay a retainer to a good yard while you go horse hunting. It gives you the peace of mind that you can move your horse straight into suitable surroundings and let him settle down, rather than having to settle for a second best yard whilst you look for a better set-up and then have to put the horse through the trauma of moving again.

Types of livery

There are five basic types of livery: DIY, full, part, grass and working. All have advantages and disadvantages, but whatever system you choose, your horse's welfare must come first.

Most people like the idea of looking after their own horses because you know that, hopefully, things will always be done the right way and it gives you a greater chance of getting to know each other. But before you commit yourself to DIY livery, be brutally realistic about how much time you can devote to your horse.

Just as important is can you give him a secure routine? Horses can and do adapt to their owners' lifestyles, but it is not fair to feed him at 7 am and 5 pm one day and 12 noon and 8 pm the next because those times fall in with your working hours.

Any owner who opts for DIY livery must have an emergency back-up system, even if they are one of the lucky few with lots of time. What happens if you fall ill, or your car breaks down and you cannot get to the stables, or you want to go on holiday? It may seem unlikely to someone in the throes of enthusiasm for horse buying, especially if this is your first venture, but there may well be a time when the idea of a week or two without mucking out seems quite attractive.

If DIY is the only option you are interested in or can afford it is essential that you have at least one friend or family member willing to learn the basics of horse management and handling. If the worst happens then at least you know someone is capable of feeding the horse, checking him for signs of injury and turning him out with the appropriate rugs on if necessary.

It is also a good idea to come to an arrangement with another owner or owners on the yard to help each other when necessary. Like-minded friends can work this out to a fine art, but it is essential that you have the same standards and are prepared to get to know the other person's horse as well as your own.

You also need to communicate with each other and trust each other's judgement. For instance, it is no good trusting someone to call out the vet in your absence, if necessary, if you have different views on what constitutes an emergency. In some cases, the yard owner will have the ultimate responsibility for all the horses kept there and the authority to take charge if disaster strikes and the horse's owner cannot be contacted, but if you rent stables and grazing from a non-horsey farmer, this may not be of any use or consolation.

Full livery is the opposite side of the coin from DIY. Taken to its extreme, it means that you could leave your horse for weeks at a time and be sure that when you see him he will be happy, healthy and well cared for. There are still a few yards where the owners announce their intentions to ride at a particular time and arrive to find their horses groomed, tacked up and waiting; when they have finished riding, they simply hand their animals to waiting stable staff and climb back in their expensive cars.

However, so few people want or can afford this sort of impersonal ownership that full livery has in most cases acquired more realistic definitions. The yard owner is responsible for the horse's daily care, which in its most basic terms means feeding, mucking out, turning out and bringing in.

If you cannot ride your horse as often as necessary, the yard staff may exercise him for you. This may comprise hacking out, lungeing or a session on a horse walker, depending on how often you are unable to ride. Most people would not want their horses lunged or put on a horse walker every day of the week, if only because of the boredom factor, but if you can ride, say, two weekdays out of five plus weekends you may be happy for him to be lunged and/or put on the walker on one or two of your away days and turned out for a rest day on the third.

Some people may prefer this sort of arrangement to having their horse hacked out, simply because they do not want anyone else riding their horse. The usual reason is that the animal is a competition horse schooled to go in a certain way and they do not want him confused or made less responsive.

There are two schools of thought on hacking: some people believe that any reasonably competent rider can do slow work round the roads on even a top-class horse, whilst others would not dream of letting anyone other than an expert rider on his back. There is also the point that many talented horses tend to have a fair amount of character and a few can be absolutely lethal for anyone but a very capable rider to hack out.

Part livery means that you and the yard share the responsibilities for looking after the horse. Some yards may be able to offer tailor-made agreements for each owner, whilst others want to keep it simple and are only prepared to give a standard service. Services offered in part livery arrangements usually involve giving feeds, turning out and bringing in, and you take care of mucking out, exercising, grooming and so on.

Part livery can be a life saver for the working owner; if you get to the yard at 7.30 am knowing that your horse was fed three-quarters of an hour before, you also know that by the time you have mucked out and are ready to ride, he will have digested his breakfast. Similarly, if you know that someone is going to bring him in at night you do not need to panic if you get delayed at work.

Grass livery is the most basic kind of all and is designed mainly for children's ponies. It means that you pay a weekly rent and in return are provided with grazing all the year round. Some yards charge a sum that includes hay when there is not enough grass, whilst others leave the provision of extra fodder to you.

However tempting the price of grass livery may seem compared to other kinds, always make sure that a stable will be available for your horse or pony in emergencies. If this means paying rent on a stable that stays empty for most of the time, accept the fact: it will only take one emergency to make you realise that what seemed like a waste of money was actually an investment.

Some yards offering grass livery insist that they worm all the animals and pass on the cost to the owners, whilst others leave it up to you. The first system has a lot to recommend it because it means that no animal slips through the net because of its owner's lack of knowledge or care. Unless the yard adds a service charge, it may also work out cheaper: for instance, wormers bought in bulk are cheaper than those purchased singly.

Working livery is a system that may sound like a good idea in theory, but in practice often causes a lot of problems. It is operated by some riding schools and the idea is that you pay a reduced livery rate in return for the school being able to use your horse or pony for its clients' lessons for so many hours per week.

The problems are that you are likely get to the stage where you do not want anyone else riding your horse—at least, not people you do not know. His schooling may also suffer because he is being ridden by lots of different people; even though his riders will be under supervision, they will still make mistakes. Asking a horse to put up with his owner's mistakes is one thing, but expecting him to put up with those of his owner and several other people a week and still remain co-operative and willing is a bit much.

Riding schools that offer well-schooled, responsive horses are able to do so for two reasons: either the horses are taken out of the school system every so often and re-tuned by experienced riders, or they are sold on to private homes before they become fed up.

The other main problem with working livery is that riding schools are busiest, and will therefore want to use your horse, at weekends. If you work during the week, this is when you will also want to ride him. As he can only work so hard, there is an inevitable clash of interests.

Choosing a yard

Many livery yard owners will invite you to look at their premises even if they do not have a current vacancy. Take advantage of this because it enables you to compare places, facilities and people.

This means that if you do have to start off in a yard that is not your top choice, you have a reference point if you get a call from another yard owner six months later asking if you are still looking. Obviously you would want to go and see the place again to make sure that there have been no drastic changes in the meantime, but you will not be left trying to remember if this was the yard with the lovely school but limited grazing or the one with good facilities and year-round turnout.

When you look at a yard, you want to see a place that gives the impression of being friendly and well-run. It does not need to look like an equestrian ideal home, though obviously it is very nice if it does. Priorities include well-maintained fields and fencing, stables that are light, well-ventilated and have adequate drainage and an owner and where applicable staff who are pleasant and conscientious.

If you want to hack out regularly and most people do even if their aims centre on competing you need to look at the surroundings as well as the yard itself. Quiet roads are becoming harder to find all the time and bridleway networks are only a dream for some riders, but however good a yard seems, do not underestimate the dangers if it is surrounded only by busy roads. Maybe there are quiet hacking areas a short box ride away, but do you have the time to travel your horse every time you want to ride out and can you afford the costs of fuel and vehicle wear and tear?

Good fencing should be high on your list of priorities when choosing a livery yard.

Take it as a good sign if the yard owner asks you as many questions as you ask them. This applies just as much, and in some cases even more, to people looking for DIY livery; whilst horsey people are usually happy to share advice and help less experienced owners, the last thing a yard owner wants is to be landed with looking after a horse without being paid for it because the owner does not know how to or cannot be bothered to care for it properly.

Explain what type of horse you are hoping to buy. If you do not mind whether you have a mare or a gelding, find out if there are already both sexes on the yard; some turn out all the horses together, whilst others have separate fields for mares and geldings. Some geldings squabble over the privilege of being a mare's special friend and if yours is the gelding who ends up getting kicked all the time or the mare who is being constantly herded away from the other horses, you might decide that segregation is a better option.

If you are prepared to buy a horse that has a stable vice, find out what the yard policy is. Some are not bothered as long as you do everything to minimise the problem, such as providing a weaving grid, whilst others operate a no stable vices policy. It has not been proven whether vices are inherited or copied or if they are triggered by various reasons, but a lot of owners of vice-free horses will not want their animals to be next to or even to see another horse weaving, crib biting or windsucking. Likewise, if you would not tolerate a horse with a stable vice and would not want your animal stabled near one, would the yard be able to accommodate this?

It is important that you and the yard owner understand exactly what you require from each other: if you decide to keep your horse at this yard, you should have a written agreement stating who is responsible for what and the exact costs. Yard owners, like everyone else, have to keep pace with rising costs so remember to ask how long the current prices will be held.

Every yard needs rules and regulations so that both horse owners and staff know where they stand. They may range from times you are welcome on the yard and those when you are not normally expected to be there to what happens in the case of an emergency. Most yard owners will reserve the right to call the vet to your horse if they think it necessary; obviously they will contact you as soon as possible, but if the horse has suspected colic and you cannot be found, immediate action may be necessary to save the horse's life.

Looking on the darkest side, the owner may also insist on authority to act on a vet's advice in your absence. If your horse is so badly injured that the vet says there is no humane alternative but for him to be destroyed, someone has to make the decision. If you cannot be contacted, that person has to be the yard owner (though in circumstances such as a road accident, a police officer can instruct a vet to destroy a fatally injured horse).

Good livery yards insist that all its residents are vaccinated against tetanus and flu. An increasing number also stipulate that horses must be insured for veterinary fees. If you put yourself in the position of a yard owner, this is fair enough. Imagine that your horse has an attack of colic. The yard owner cannot contact you, but calls the vet who says that surgery offers the only hope of saving the horse and the alternative is to put him down. The cost of such an operation will be £2,000 plus: if you are not insured and the yard owner does not know whether you would be able or prepared to pay such a sum, how does she make a decision?

Some yard owners ask clients to sign an agreement detailing who is responsible for what and setting out any rules. This is a good idea because it helps to avoid any misunderstandings. If the yard does not issue agreements, you can draw up your own. At least one firm of solicitors with a specialist in equestrian litigation will draw up an agreement for you according to your particular circumstances.

Chapter 8
Finding and Viewing a Horse

At long last, you are ready to start looking for your horse. It may seem to have taken a long time to get this far, but good preparation saves time, money and tempers in the long run.

Specialist magazines and local publications are a good source of 'horses for sale' adverts.

There are several ways of finding out about horses for sale. Advertisements in specialist horse magazines, notably *Horse and Hound*, *Horse Exchange* and *Your Horse*, are always a good avenue. Do not ignore local papers or the free ads publications: it may be a sign of horse owners' reluctance to spend money, but the latter often carry hefty sections of horses for sale adverts. Specialist magazines will also carry details of forthcoming sales, so if you are considering this approach you can send off for auctioneers' catalogues.

You can also make inquiries with good dealers, though be prepared to be asked at least as many and maybe more questions than you pose. The dealer is actually doing you a favour by this, as his time is money and he will not want to waste it showing you a horse you can neither ride nor afford. He also will not want the horse to be ridden by more unknown quantities than necessary.

Most people start reading for sale advertisements long before they are actually ready to buy a horse. You may already have been filled with enthusiasm for horses who seem to be just what you are looking for, but you now need to turn a more discerning eye to your search.

Exciting as it may be, you also need to be calm and methodical in your approach. Start by finalising in your own mind exactly what you want to do, what sort of horse you would like, what you could put up with and what would be unacceptable and how much you can afford to pay. Most people put prices in their adverts, and whilst they may well negotiate, this will only be within reasonable limits.

For instance, whilst someone who advertises a horse at £3,250 may be prepared to take £3,000 in some circumstances, they are unlikely to be happy if your maximum price is £2,500. There are also plenty of people who set a price on a take it or leave it basis, in which case you either take it, leave it, or hope that the lack of a better offer may encourage them to reconsider.

Auctioneers' catalogues do not offer price guidelines, but if you read sales reports and/or go to a couple to get an idea of going rates, you should be able to work out your own. Unless the sale is a prestigious one, prices will usually be lower than in the private sector—but you have to accept all the inherent risks of buying at auction, as explained earlier.

It is also sensible to decide how far you are prepared to travel. Some people will travel the length and breadth of the country to look at a likely sounding horse, but most find that only an exceptional prospect is worth more than a two-hour drive. The situation may be different if you can arrange to see more than one horse in the same area; perhaps a dealer has two or three on offer, or there is more than one likely sounding advert.

One way round the problem is to ask owners of likely sounding horses who are a long distance away if they would send you some photographs, but you do of course run the risk of someone else seeing it and buying it first in which case, remember that there is always another horse on another day. Good photographs that give a clear idea of the horse's conformation cannot, of course, indicate his temperament or movement—though you may be able to tell if, for instance, he is likely to brush—but they may help you decide whether to gamble on a long journey.

There is an encouraging trend for adverts to be accompanied by photographs, which at least gives you some idea of what you are going to look at. It may be amusing to see advertisement copy describing a stunning event prospect accompanied by a photograph of a long-backed, cow-hocked horse with a dipped back, but that is infinitely preferable to travelling 100 miles to see it.

You will soon learn to read not only the adverts and sales descriptions, but also between the lines. Common sense dictates that a vendor will want to emphasise the horse's good points and minimise its bad ones, so look at what has not been said as well as what is and remember to check those points if you ring up to find out more.

For instance, if the advert describes a horse as good to box, clip and shoe, is he also good in traffic? If he is said to be good in all respects, check that you do not have more considerations than the vendor. Similarly, ask questions about the horse who is good to shoe, box etc; you might think that being good in traffic is an essential etcetera, but the vendor might not.

It is a good idea to make a list of questions and keep them by the phone whenever you inquire about a horse. That way you can be sure you have not missed a vital point and committed yourself to looking at a horse that further questioning would have revealed as unsuitable.

The following list of suggested questions may help. They will not all be vital to every purchaser, so you will have to adapt your list as necessary.

1.   Double check the horse's height, even though it will have been stated in the advertisement. Has the vendor measured the horse, or are they guessing? Unfortunately, a lot of people are wildly inaccurate about estimating height. If the horse has not been measured correctly, be prepared for the risk of seeing a supposed 15.2hh who is struggling to get over 15hh, and so on.

If a maximum height is vital, usually because you are looking for a show horse or pony, check whether the animal has a current height certificate under the Joint Measurement Scheme. Four, five and six-year-olds have to be measured annually, so you may have to decide whether or not to take the risk on a four-year-old who is already up to height continuing to measure in as he matures. If no certificate is available, check whether the owner would agree a sale subject to a height certificate being given.

2.   Be similarly careful about the horse's age. Is the owner guessing, going by dentition or by breed registration documents? A lot of horses seem to get to nine or ten years old and then stop.

3.   Is the horse's breeding known? If so, does the owner have the appropriate breed society documents? In some circumstances, such as buying a child's first pony, you may not be concerned about its breeding. But if you are buying a mare you later hope to breed from yourself, or a horse to show in breed classes, you will be wasting your time without them.

4.   If the breeding is unknown, what type is the horse or pony? Here again you may have to keep your fingers crossed, as some definitions of a lightweight, middleweight or cob may not turn out to be the same as yours.

5.   Is he good in traffic? Hopefully the answer will be a straightforward 'Yes,' but if there are any qualifications such as 'He's good with most things but doesn't always like lorries/tractors/motor bikes' you have to decide whether your circumstances would make this horse a safe bet for you.

6.   Does he have any stable vices does he weave, windsuck or crib bite? If the answer is 'No,' all well and good. If the vendor tells you that the horse does have a vice, but only to a small degree and in certain circumstances, you again have to decide whether or not you can accept it. Remember that if it has been admitted, however slight the degree is made out to be, you have no comeback if you get the horse home and it weaves like a top through all the daylight hours.

7. Does he have any allergies? A horse with a dust allergy or sweet itch will be more difficult and perhaps more expensive to manage.

8. Is he good to catch, shoe, box, clip and load? To a certain extent, you have to accept the vendor's word here though you can always ask to see the horse caught out of the field, or loaded into a horsebox or trailer.

Of all these problems, difficulty in clipping is the one most people would find most acceptable. With professional help, there are usually ways round it. A horse that is difficult to shoe, though, demands a patient, understanding farrier: unfortunately this is not a failing most owners would admit, unless you are buying locally and the horse is well known for the problem or you and the owner share the same farrier.

9. Will he hack out alone as happily as in company? This may be important to you, but if the owner says he does not know because the horse is never asked to do this, you will have to ask him to find out and be prepared to demonstrate it to you if necessary.

10. If you want to compete, does the horse have a competition record? If he has winnings in affiliated competitions, ask his registered name and check both his description and his winnings with the relevant organising body.

11. What sort of bit is he ridden in? If you want to compete in the lower levels of dressage, the horse will have to be ridden in one of the permitted snaffle bits. Most horses can be schooled to go nicely in one of these on the flat, but if the horse is routinely ridden in a gag snaffle with a Grakle noseband, you will have your work cut out.

12. Is he freeze-marked? If so, make a note of the number if you visit the horse and check with the freeze-marking company that he is not on the stolen register. It has been known to happen, and causes a lot of heartbreak. The buyer is usually the person who loses out.

Your detective work will eventually pay dividends, and you will be able to turn theory into practice by going to look at horses that sound suitable. Try not to be too disheartened if it takes some time: weeding out the no-hopers at the start is a lot better than wasting your, and the seller's, time by taking the process a stage further.

Make sure you have good directions on how to get there; it might sound obvious, but it is all too easy to spend an hour driving round an unsignposted rural area looking for a stableyard, even though 'you can't miss it'! Be definite about times because people's idea of 'about two o'clock' vary.

Looking at a horse can be divided into five sections: first impressions, in the stable, examining him on the yard, seeing his owner ride him and finally riding him yourself.

First impressions

When meeting someone for the first time you form an immediate impression of whether you are going to like them or not, and the same applies with a horse. In both cases, first impressions can sometimes be accurate and sometimes misleading, so do not look at the horse over the stable door and condemn him unless he is obviously different from his description (and if you have done your homework properly, this should not happen).

Remember that you are seeing a horse on his own territory, where he feels safe and relaxed. Do not worry if he seems a bit dozy and quiet; in fact, that can be a good sign. If he is standing in the corner poised for flight, you may have a problem!

Notice how he is standing. Lots of horses rest a hind leg, but if he is obviously pointing a foot, especially in front, it could be a sign that something is wrong. When you open the door and walk in, does he seem interested and reasonably friendly? Do his ears flick forwards or does he put them back and threaten you? Even worse, does he present you with his backside and hint that if you come any farther he will kick?

You should be able to approach him quietly without him showing any sign of fear or temper. Put a hand on his girth area and make him move over to see that he can turn. If his response is to barge you out of the way, you know you are faced with a bad-mannered animal who is either young and uneducated or has learned that he can impose his will on people rather than the other way round.

If the horse is freeze-marked, you can check whether he has ever been reported as stolen.

While you are assessing his conformation, notice if he is freeze-marked. If so, make a mental note of the number and check it later with the freeze-marking company. They will be able to tell you whether or not the horse has been reported as stolen, which may sound suspicious on your part, but is a worthwhile check. If you buy a stolen horse, albeit unwittingly, you are likely to end up the loser.

If you are buying a very young horse—a just weaned foal, or a yearling, two or three-year-old—it may be harder to assess him unless you have experience of seeing horses develop. All foals are cute and cuddly and as they grow up they go through a sometimes erratic growth process that can make them look out of proportion.

Yearlings and three-year-olds are the worst in this respect, as they will often be higher at one end than the other. Two-year-olds tend to settle down for a time, then go back to being ugly ducklings. All you can do is use your judgement and keep your fingers crossed that the ugly duckling will eventually turn into a swan.

However, even with a gangly youngster you will be able to judge the quality of his limbs and movement and tell what sort of temperament he has. Apply the same conformation guidelines as you would to an older horse: good joints, short cannon bones, pasterns not too upright and so on. Avoid youngsters who are so narrow in the chest that they look as if both front legs come out of the same hole because they will be uncomfortable to ride, often lack strength and stamina and often move badly.

As far as temperament goes, young horses tend to be naturally curious. If he comes up to see you when you walk into his field, all well and good, though you have to take into account how much he has been handled. What you do not want to see is a youngster who lays back his ears and threatens to bite or kick you.

Trotting up

So far, so good? If you are looking at a mature horse, ask to see him brought out of the stable and trotted up immediately. A lot of people will inspect a horse's conformation first, but it is a good idea to see him move from a cold start to see if he is stiff or even unlevel. We are presupposing that he has not been exercised that day; if someone has been to look at him earlier, just bear it in mind.

You want to see him led on a slack rein, so that his movement is as natural as possible. Start by standing behind and watching him walk away from and then back towards you. Ideally you should see a nice free walk with a generous stride; racehorse trainers judge yearlings on the way they walk because a horse that walks well will usually have a good gallop. Ideally the imprints of the hind feet should overtrack the imprints of the forefeet by four to eight inches.

Next ask to see him trot, again on a slack rein. To really assess a horse you need to see him trotted up four times, while you watch from the front, back, nearside and offside. Your first task is to assess whether the horse is level and sound: if not, there is no point in going on! Trot is the pace that will reveal any irregularities in movement whether the horse dishes, brushes or plaits.

Dishing means that the horse throws out one or both forelegs from the knee. Brushing is when one fetlock brushes against the other, and can occur in front or behind. Plaiting means that the horse crosses one foot over the other, usually in front. Any irregularity is a weakness because it puts extra strain on the limbs and the horse is more likely to injure himself and possibly fall, but you do not necessarily have to turn a horse down if he does not move straight. It depends how bad the defect is and what you want him for; a show hack that dishes will never get anywhere, but a show jumper that moves slightly askew might be quite acceptable.

A horse should ideally move straight when trotted up.

Good movement means that the horse is more likely to stay on his feet and be a comfortable ride. He will cover more ground with each stride and so be more economical in the effort his limbs are subjected to, and will move freely and in a good rhythm. His joints will flex properly and he will put his feet firmly on the ground.

If you are looking at an unbroken horse, it is nice to see him move loose in the field as well as being trotted up. Apply the same criteria, remembering that a horse who moves badly as a yearling or two-year-old is not going to improve with age.

On the yard

Now it is time to judge the horse's make and shape, and if you feel confident enough, to get an idea of his age. The owner may show you registration papers, so do make sure that they belong to this horse! The best guide is the picture, as it is colloquially called, on a vaccination certificate: this is marked by a veterinary surgeon with detailed markings, including whorls. As a horse's whorl pattern is as unique as a person's fingerprint, an expert can check one against the other and your vet will do this when you eventually get to the stage of the pre-purchase examination.

This horse dishes on his near fore, but it would not necessarily bother someone who wanted a show jumper, hunter or eventer.

You will need to look in the horse's mouth to check that he is not drastically overshot or undershot, so checking his age can be done at the same time. It is something your vet will cover, though strictly speaking a horse over eight years is technically known as aged. The vet should be able to make an accurate guess at the age of an older horse, even though recent research suggests that dentition is not such a reliable guide as we have always assumed.

Ageing by dentition is a mixture of looking at the markings on the teeth and the length and shape of the incisors. A horse's first set of teeth are the milk teeth, and these are replaced at varying intervals by the permanent ones.

A yearling has a complete set of milk incisors, which are white and straight. Between two and two-and-a-half, depending on his growth, the central incisors change and between three and three-and-a-half the outside incisors (laterals) are replaced by permanents. The next change appears between three-and-a-half and four, when he gets the permanent corner incisors, and at five he is said to have a full mouth with the corner incisors coming into wear.

Tushes, small teeth set back from the incisors, are another indication of a male horse's age and usually appear at about four-and-a-half. They are small and sharp and rarely cause any problems: do not confuse them with wolf teeth, which often do. Wolf teeth are found usually in the front of the upper jaw, about half to one inch away from the front of the molars, and very occasionally in the lower one. They can cause bitting problems, but are easily removed, and you can find them in mares as well as geldings.

When a horse is five or over look at the black marks in the centre flat surfaces (tables) of his teeth. As he gets older, so they get smaller through wear and tear. The marks disappear first from the central teeth, then from the laterals and finally from the corners.

At six, the horse's corner incisors will meet and be in full wear and at seven, a noticeable hook appears on the corner teeth. At nine there is a pronounced triangular formation in the centres of the teeth, which gradually becomes more oval. The teeth become longer as the horse gets older, hence the expression 'long in the tooth.'

The next commonly used indicator of age is the Galvayne's groove. This is a brownish groove on the outside of the upper corner incisors and is used to age a horse between ten and twenty years old. It starts when the horse is ten, reaches halfway down the tooth at about fifteen and gets to the bottom when he is about twenty. It then grows out, if the horse lives long enough.

Registration papers may show the horse's actual birthday, but for official purposes this is January 1 for all Thoroughbreds and May 1 for half-bred horses.

When examining the teeth, check the front ones for signs of extra wear; it could mean that the horse is a crib biter, though of course the owner should have disclosed this. It is possible to give a false age by bishoping, where the teeth are filed and marked to make the horse look younger, but this also takes off the enamel and when the horse's mouth is closed his teeth will not meet evenly. The process is named after a vet, Mr Bishop, who discovered in 1884 that the teeth of a Derby runner had been tampered with in this way.

Once you are satisfied that the horse's teeth seem to correspond to his stated age, ask to see him standing square on reasonably level ground. Stand about two yards away and remember our blueprint for good conformation.

Start at the front and work your way back. Now that the horse has been brought out of his box he should look reasonably alert and interested in what is going on around him, with ears forward.

When you stand in front of him, does he have enough chest room or do both his legs come out of the same hole? His knees should be at the same height and look as if they are a pair; white hairs or scars are a sign of broken (blemished) knees and could mean that the horse habitually falls over. His feet should also be a pair, and when you move to the side check whether he is standing level or if he favours a foot.

Again from the side, you should watch the horse breathing. There should be a single inspiration and expiration; double breathing is usually a sign that the horse has a wind problem. His hocks should be nearly perpendicular, with no protuberances such as curbs that signify weakness. If he does have a curb, is it a true one or a false one? Pick up the affected leg or legs: a false curb will disappear but a true one will still be all too visible. Stand behind him and look at his hips. They should be level and equal, not dropping down on one side.

Return to the side and feel his legs. Your questioning should have forewarned you of any lumps, bumps and blemishes: if a horse is described as clean-legged there should be no bony protuberances, swellings or scars. Run your hands down the cannon bones on his forelegs and feel for any splints; these are bony lumps that rarely cause soundness problems once formed unless they interfere with the action of the knee. Splints can appear on the hind legs, but they are not as common.

Feel round the fetlocks and coronets for signs of ringbone, a bony formation that is categorised as either high or low; high ringbone is easier to feel. It is usually caused by concussion on hard ground, but can be hereditary or the result of a blow. Whatever the reason, do not buy the horse.

The back of the heel should be soft enough for you to press it in with your finger. If it is hard, with no give, the horse probably has a sidebone ossification of the foot cartilages. A horse usually goes lame when a sidebone is forming, but then often comes sound.

There are some conditions, such as navicular disease, which can only be identified with nerve blocks and X-rays (though the horse will of course be lame). Even then, interpreting X-rays is a job for a specialist. It often first shows up when the horse is worked on a circle, and trotting him in a circle on concrete can show signs of an early problem; your vet may also carry out a flexion test in his pre-purchase vetting that can warn of any dangers in this area.

Look at the horse's feet. Do they make two matching pairs, front and hind, or is one foot in each pair a different shape and/or size from its partner? Some horses have mismatched feet and never have any problems, but in others it can be an indicator of trouble to come.

If the problem is marked, you need to be cautious. If you really like him in all other respects, you may decide to mention your worries to your vet when you arrange a pre-purchase vetting and take his advice from there.

Joints take a great deal of stress. The biggest and most powerful joint is the hock, which can house all sorts of problems. A horse that moves well does so not from the front, but from behind: his engine is in his hind legs and sends him powering forwards. You do not want to see a horse drag his hocks or leave them behind; they should be placed well underneath him.

A bog spavin is unsightly, but a bone spavin is much more worrying. If you pick up the hind leg, flex the hock joint for thirty seconds and then ask the horse to trot on straight away, he may go lame if a bone spavin is present. Your vet will carry out this test as part of his examination.

Stringhalt is another problem to watch out for. This affects the adductor muscles and causes one hind leg to be lifted much higher than the other. It often gets worse as the horse gets older, and whilst surgery may improve some mild cases, there is no cure. You may only see it for a few strides in the early stages, but if you suspect it, ask to see the horse backed up in hand and then trotted off. It should show more clearly when he moves off and some horses with stringhalt cannot back up at all.

A horse with bowed hocks may well brush or speedy cut when he moves. Speedy cutters can injure their hocks, cannon bones or knees, depending on whether they knock their legs in front or behind.

Look at the horse's musculature. Is he reasonably symmetrical, or is there noticeable wastage on the croup or in the stifle area? Sometimes you see wastage just on one side, whilst at other times both can be affected.

Muscle wastage on one side is usually a sign of an old injury, whilst general lack of muscle development means that the horse has either never been worked properly or has been worked incorrectly. Bear in mind the horse's age: you cannot expect a just backed three-year-old to show the same developed musculature as a correctly schooled mature horse.

Do not confuse fat with muscle. Fat can conceal a multitude of sins to the novice eye, so if you cannot tell the difference, make sure you bring along someone who can.

Seeing him ridden

If you have come this far and are still interested, ask to see the horse tacked up and ridden. You may have a doubt or two but still be interested; in this case, carry on. But if at any time during the procedure you think that this is definitely not the horse for you, say so and avoid wasting everyone's time.

A polite 'Thanks very much, he's very nice but not quite what I'm looking for' should not offend anyone. There is no need to pull a horse to bits, whether the criticisms you make are justified or an attempt to get the price down. If the owner is knowledgeable, they will already be aware of the horse's defects; if they mean nothing, your words will have no meaning. In any case, such criticism is simply rudeness.

Occasionally you may meet an owner who takes the fact that you are not interested in buying the horse personally and will ask you what you think is wrong with him, perhaps in an aggrieved or slightly belligerent way. The best way out of this situation is simply to repeat that you have definite requirements and this horse does not quite match up to them. If you feel it necessary to point out that the animal has two great big splints, is narrow in the chest, sickle-hocked and pigeon-toed, that is up to you, but inviting such discussion is usually a waste of time.

Ask a few questions while the horse is being tacked up. Is the bit the one that he is normally ridden in (and does it match up with the information you were given at your first inquiries?). You should also notice whether or not the tack fits properly; it is amazing how many people use bits that are the wrong size (usually too big) and fitted incorrectly (usually too low). Similarly, ill-fitting saddles can cause discomfort and back problems.

Observe the horse's general attitude. Does he stay relaxed and co-operative, or does he clamp his jaw and throw his head up to evade the bridle? Many horses chomp the bit when first bridled, but any mouth evasions being ridden, such as trying to put his tongue over the bit (or succeeding!) can cause serious problems. A three or four-year-old who is cutting teeth may show mouth resistances because of discomfort.

A well-mannered horse will stand still when mounted and not need someone to hold him or stand by his head. If he is cold-backed and dips away from the rider's weight at first, you should be warned about this. Watch the rider's technique: does he use a mounting block, take a leg-up, or heave himself up from the ground, pulling the saddle to one side in the process? If the latter applies, the horse may well fidget or try to walk off as the rider gets on, and who could blame him?

If the vendor has good facilities he might first take the horse into an indoor or outdoor school. Watch what he does with the horse: you want the chance to see all his paces. If the rider goes into trot straight away it might be because the horse has a poor walk (which you should have spotted when you saw him led up). Similarly, if he goes straight from walk to canter it could be an attempt to minimise a bad quality trot.

Make sure you see the horse worked on both reins in all paces. Most horses are stiffer to one side than another, just as we are left- or right-handed, and it is perfectly acceptable to start by working the horse on his good rein. But as he loosens up, he should be worked equally on both.

Many people like to see a horse ridden in the open as well as in an enclosed area. Seeing him in the school should give you an idea of how well-schooled or green he is, whether he strikes off on the correct canter lead and is generally well-balanced, supple and obedient (though obviously the rider needs to be capable of pressing the right buttons). If he performs as well or nearly as well in an open field he has learned his lessons; some horses become distracted in the open and ride much greener when they do not have the support of the school walls or fence.

You will want to see the horse galloped, not to see how fast he can go but to spot any wind defects. A broken-winded horse will show the characteristic double heave of the flanks when standing, as mentioned earlier. Seeing him galloped also gives you an idea of how good his brakes are—it is better to watch someone else being tanked off than to experience it yourself!

Listen to the horse's breathing when he gallops and when he pulls up. Is he a high blower, due to excessive flapping of the false nostril, or a roarer (much more serious and caused by an affliction of the larynx)? The other noise to listen for is whistling, a higher note than roaring. It is due to paralysis of the left side of the larynx and is usually caused by a virus or strangles. Generally, a noise on expiration is nothing to worry about, but a noise on inspiration is.

Nasal discharge is an associated sign that something is wrong, but is not usually permanent. For instance, a watery discharge can be an indicator of equine flu.

Unless you are buying a horse purely for dressage or showing, you need to see him jump. A horse will inevitably jump better for someone who knows him, and who he is used to, than he will for a stranger. This is the owner's chance to show you what he can do, and if he puts him over some big fences you should not necessarily do the same yourself or worry that you might be expected to.

Finally, double check that the horse is traffic proof and is happy to leave the yard on his own before preparing to ride him yourself.

Riding the horse

Now is your chance to confirm the impressions you have built up about the horse. If it makes you feel more confident, get someone to stand by his head while you mount: you have already seen whether or not he stands still and do not need it proving again.

Walk on, get the feel of the horse and then go into trot. Do you feel comfortable on the horse? Are you happy and comfortable? Do you feel that you want to carry on riding him? You will soon build an impression by doing a few quiet transitions and circles on either rein; if you do not like the feel of the horse (and it may be that he simply does not give the sort of ride you like) then come gently back to halt and say so.

As long as you feel happy, you can carry on. Make sure the horse is happy, too; do not take a strong hold on the reins and then kick him in the ribs to see how he reacts. Let the horse go freely forwards; when you get on a strange horse you do not say 'You will do this,' but rather ask 'Please will you do this?'

How much you ask obviously depends on the horse's age and experience. An older, well-schooled horse may well come on to the bit and show some lateral work, but the owner should have already demonstrated this. Few riders can ride a strange horse and get the best out of him straight away, and it is important to remember that a horse is an animal, not a machine: he needs to get used to you as much as you need to get used to him.

If all goes well, you will be able to walk, trot and canter the horse quite happily and obtain reasonable transitions from one pace to another and back again. Then ask to try him over a cross-pole; approach it in a rhythmic trot, without pushing the horse out of balance, and let him sort out his own stride. Be prepared to listen to the person who is showing him to you, because he knows the horse.

Providing you feel confident, you can canter into a small upright fence, which for the average horse and rider should be no more than two foot nine inches high. Approach it in a balanced, rhythmic canter and let the fence come to you; the horse should be able to sort himself out over this height. Is he as willing to jump going away from home as he is towards it?

The specialist show jumper will be looking for a horse with a particularly good jumping technique, one which lifts its forearms in front and is equally careful behind. Ideally, the horse will bascule—make a round shape over the fence rather than jumping with a hollow back and his head in the air.

If the horse has a good competition record with current winnings, you will probably need to do no more than jump him yourself at the height you intend to start competing at and ask the seller to show him performing over something bigger. If you have any doubts or want further evidence of the horse's ability, ask to see him go through a double and treble and/or jump a fence with water trays underneath if this should be within his experience.

Occasionally you may find that the seller has minimal or even inadequate facilities. If you like the horse but are unable to see him give an adequate performance, the seller should be prepared to take him somewhere with better facilities—perhaps a local yard or show centre with good going and adequate fences. It is up to the owner to take the horse there, but the cost of hiring the facilities will be down to you.

If the horse is supposed to be an experienced competition animal and the owner is reluctant to show him to you anywhere other than in a boggy field with two oil drums and three poles, you have to ask yourself if he might have a problem. Taking a gamble on such a horse, however well he jumps over the aforesaid poles and two oil drums, would not be sensible.

Assessing an unbroken or recently broken horse's jumping potential takes an expert eye and a bit of luck. If a four-year-old jumps in good style over a two foot fence, he will hopefully do the same over a bigger one. But if he dangles his front legs and consistently forgets about his back ones, jumping will perhaps not be his forte!

It does not matter if a horse has a fence down—they all do this sometimes. What does matter is the way he approaches it next time round. It is always a good sign if he makes an extra effort to clear it, but if he repeats his mistake and obviously could not care less, you are fighting a losing battle.

An unbroken three-year-old who is being marketed as a potential jumper should be seen loose-schooled or lunged over a fence. If what you see is encouraging, all well and good, but you have to accept that there is still a risk factor. Some horses make a fantastic show over a fence loose, but never manage the same with a rider on board. Conversely, there are also a few who fall over their first tiny fences and then suddenly realise what it is about and surprise everyone.

On the roads

The final test, if you are still happy with the horse, is to ride him on the roads. You should normally be accompanied by another rider, as you are on a strange horse and probably in a strange place. Put yourself in the seller's position: would you allow a complete stranger to go off alone on your horse? However, you also need to make sure that the horse is happy to go alone and is not dependent on others. Nappy horses are not worth the stable room they take up.

While you are out, vary your position both going away from home and returning. Let the other rider go in front; you must expect your horse to want to keep up, but he should not get silly and start pulling, jogging on the spot or crabbing sideways. How does he react to the other horse? You can put up with a bit of face pulling, but be careful about the horse who lunges at a companion with teeth bared. Similarly, when you go in front your companion should keep a reasonable distance behind, but if he is extra cautious, does it mean that your horse is likely to kick?

When you take the lead, your horse should be perfectly happy: no hanging back or becoming suddenly spooky. The final test comes when returning to the yard: ask your companion to go in, but ask your horse to walk past the entrance on his own. You can forgive a horse, particularly a young one, for a slight hesitation, but he should still walk on when you ask him to. Any marked reluctance, or worse still an attempt to whip round and/or rear, is an indication of nappiness.

By now you should have a good idea of whether you like the horse enough to buy it, and some people may make their minds up there and then. Others prefer to make a second visit, especially if they want to bring along someone more knowledgeable. Few sellers will quibble with that, but it is only fair to make your return visit as soon as possible (and to realise that you risk losing the horse to anyone who sees him in the meantime and is prepared to make a firm commitment).

You might be tempted to ask if you can have the horse on trial for a week or a fortnight, but few sellers will agree—and with good reason. After all, would you let a stranger take away your valuable horse, knowing that he might not look after him or ride him as well as you do? It also means that the horse is unavailable to other potential buyers, and if the trial is unsuccessful the seller has to go to the expense of advertising him again.

Buyers' responsibilities

There are a lot of stories about unscrupulous sellers, but anyone who has ever sold a horse can probably tell you a few stories about nightmare buyers, too. Make sure you do not come into this category, even if only inadvertently.

If you are not in a position to buy a horse, or cannot afford to buy it, do not go and look at it. If you do, you are nothing more than a joyrider. A lot of people do this, giving the excuse that they are just seeing what is on the market, but it is inexcusable.

When you make arrangements to see a horse, stick to them as closely as you can. No one can help being held up in traffic, or getting lost, but if you know you are going to be very late, the least you can do is ring up and leave a message. If the place where the horse is kept does not have a phone there may be nothing you can do, but if there is a contact number, use it.

There is no point in deliberately arriving half-an-hour early thinking you will catch out a seller who has something to disguise. A lame horse will still be lame, and anyone who intends to lunge a horse for two hours before you get there will have done it long before.

If you want to take someone with you, tell the vendor beforehand. No one should object to you bringing a knowledgeable friend or instructor, but it is not fair to arrive with a committee in tow. Similarly, few people will mind if you want to video the horse in action but you should always ask first. Some people may get nervous about being put under scrutiny like this and feel they will not be able to show the horse off to its best advantage, in which case you can ask your helper simply to video you riding.

When you ride the horse, think of it as meeting someone for the first time. You are looking for common ground, not setting out to antagonise him so that you can see what his reaction is. With an experienced horse, you should expect to be able to carry a jumping whip or one of the shorter schooling ones, but a particularly long schooling whip is out of place. Even a shorter one should be out of bounds if you are not absolutely positive that you will not tap or flick the horse by accident.

Treat him with the respect you should give to any horse, no matter how quiet he is said to be. Fasten your coat, rather than let it flap around; mount from a mounting block if one is available; keep your aids as quiet as possible.

Formalities

At last, you have made up your mind and decided that this is the horse you want to buy. You have every reason to feel cheerful but do not start celebrating yet.

Make sure that as soon as you are ready to say that you would like to buy the horse (subject to a successful veterinary examination) you are able to pay a deposit. Some sellers will not ask for one and may be surprised when you offer, but others will insist. The amount required varies from seller to seller; some ask from £50 up to £100 simply as a token of good faith, whereas others will want 10 per cent of the purchase price. The way the deposit is paid also depends on the seller's preference, as some will ask for cash and others will accept a cheque.

Why ask for a deposit at all? Quite simply, it is to discourage people from saying they want to buy one horse, then ringing up a day or so later because they have changed their minds and found another. Every buyer has the prerogative of changing his mind, but he should be prepared to pay for it by forfeiting his deposit to compensate the seller for lost time and other potential sales and the cost of re-advertising.

In theory, paying a deposit also protects you from the seller who agrees a price with you and then rings up to announce that someone else has offered a higher one and that if you want the horse, you will have to match it. When you pay a deposit and get a written receipt for it, you have entered into a contract with the seller.

In practice, if the above situation arises and the seller sends back your deposit, the only way you could try and get recompense would be through legal action. Most people in this situation would probably feel that it was not worth the hassle, but you would have the option of trying to get compensation for your time and travelling expenses.

The receipt for your deposit should carry the name and address of the person issuing it and also of the person to whom it is issued, and could be worded as follows:

Received on (date) a deposit of £X on the 16.2hh hands six-year-old bay gelding known as Whatta Bargain. (Amend as necessary.) This deposit is taken subject to a full veterinary examination, which may include X-rays and blood tests. Should this veterinary examination be unsuccessful, the deposit will be returned in full. Should the sale not be concluded for any other reason, the deposit will be forfeit.

This agreement should be signed by both buyer and seller and it is then up to you, as the buyer, to arrange for a veterinary examination. Normally this should be done within five working days of you agreeing to buy the horse, unless there is a good reason for a delay (such as you or the vendor going on holiday).

Remember that the horse belongs to the person selling it until you have actually handed over the full price in cash or your cheque has been cleared. This last transaction is made on completion of a successful veterinary examination: the final hurdle.

Chapter 9
Pre-purchase Vetting

It is essential to have a horse or pony vetted before completing your purchase. Some people claim that it is not worth it, especially in the case of a young or cheap animal but this argument does not stand up. A knowledgeable horse person may well be able to judge a horse's conformation and ability and be able to make an accurate guess on its soundness, but only a vet can tell if an animal has a hidden problem such as a heart murmur or an eye defect.

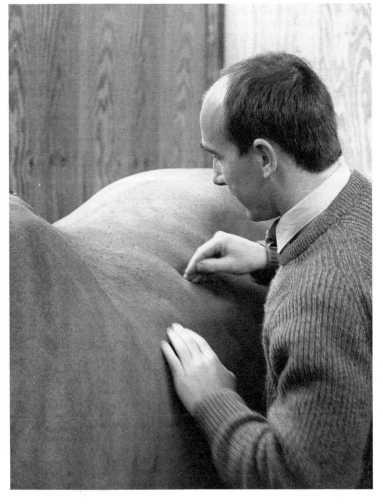

Pre-purchase vetting is a job that demands a specialist horse vet. The vet will examine the horse for any clinical signs of illness or injury that may prevent him from doing the job you require him for. Hopefully you will not be disappointed!

If you intend to insure the horse (usually a sensible move) you will find that many insurance companies require a veterinary certificate for animals valued at more than a certain amount. Even when this is not a specific requirement, it can give you extra protection if problems develop later: if your horse develops respiratory problems nine months after you bought him, a veterinary certificate showing that there were no indications at the time of purchase may save you having to argue whether or not it was a pre-existing condition.

Even if you are buying a £300 pony for your child, you will find that the £150 or so it costs you to have the animal vetted will be a good investment. Supposing you simply hand over the money and take the pony home, not realising that he has a heart defect, and he collapses a few months later while your child is riding him? At the very least, you run the risk of the defect that a vet would have spotted on his pre-purchase examination showing up later, resulting at best in inconvenience and expense and at worst in heartbreak.

A satisfactory vet's report also gives you peace of mind, which is worth quite a lot in itself. It confirms your opinion that the horse is suitable for your purpose and greatly reduces the risk of spending time and money on an animal that proves to be incapable of the work you want him to do because of an unsoundness.

The examination procedure is so methodical and has become so widely accepted that the phrase to vet has actually passed into the English language. In this case it means the vet will make a clinical examination of the horse to detect signs of injury and/or disease and provide an expert opinion on whether the horse is suitable for your purpose: in other words, whether they recommend purchase.

It is human nature to want things in black and white, with no grey areas. Unfortunately that cannot be applied to vetting: you have to accept that it is a vet's opinion based on the particular day on which he saw the horse. That is not meant to devalue the worth of the pre-purchase examination, but it does mean you need to choose your vet carefully and make sure he understands exactly what you will be expecting from the horse.

All vets undergo a lengthy training that qualifies them to examine and treat all kinds of animals, but once qualified they tend to specialise in small animals (dogs, cats, etc) or large ones, notably horses and farm animals. So whereas any vet will be qualified to make a pre-purchase examination for you, it makes sense to ask a horse vet (rather than a cat and dog one) to do it for you. He will have experience of dealing with horses and will have a better base of knowledge on which to form an opinion. As we already know, there is no such thing as a perfect horse; a good horse vet will not only be able to spot defects, but will be able to advise you on whether or not they can be disregarded or are likely to affect the animal.

A veterinary certificate is not a warranty, it is an opinion of an animal's suitability and soundness which is the best you can get! It is valid only on the day of the examination, so while a seller may tell you in all truth and honesty that the horse passed the vet with flying colours a year ago or even a month ago, you should never rely on an old certificate. With horses, a lot can happen in a short while.

Similarly, do not be satisfied with a vet's certificate produced by the seller, even if it is dated in the last few days. The Royal College of Veterinary Surgeons and the Royal Veterinary Association state that they are clear that the proper person to examine a horse prior to a change of ownership is the vet appointed by the potential purchaser or his agent. They say that serious difficulties have been encountered in the past regarding certification of horses for sale, especially by auction, to persons unknown and for an unknown purpose.

When you ask a vet to examine a horse his responsibility is to you, his client. It can be awkward if you buy a horse locally and find that you and the vendor normally use the same veterinary practice because some vets might feel it puts them in a no win position. The best thing to do in this situation is to ask him to recommend someone from another horse practice: this is fair to both sides, as you get an impartial view.

If the seller is willing for you to use the vet that he also uses, there is no reason why this cannot go ahead. But if he objects to this, usually because he feels the vet will not be able to be impartial, you have to decide whether or not to ask a different vet to do the job. It has to be said that warning bells may also ring in your mind as to whether the horse has had problems in the past that the first vet treated.

There is nothing to stop you asking the seller if this is why he wants you to choose a different vet, but there is no guarantee on the answer you will get. The horse may, of course, have been treated successfully for a one-off problem, or he may be up for sale because the vendor does not want to risk a recurrence.

You may occasionally find that a seller does not want his horses examined by a particular vet. At the end of the day, the choice of vet is down to you and if the seller does not like it, they either put up with it or lose a sale.

Your vet's job is to recommend or advise against purchase purely on the grounds stipulated earlier. He is not there to tell you whether or not he thinks the horse will make a Grade A show jumper or whether he thinks it moves well enough to do dressage, though obviously he will point out conformation and movement defects. Nor will he tell you if he thinks the horse's temperament makes him unsuitable for you though he will note anything he notices during his examination, such as a horse that naps while being ridden or tries to kick him when he runs his hand down its hind legs.

Stable vices do not form part of the veterinary examination, though the vet will record if he notices the horse weaving or behaving in any other objectionable manner. It is up to you to get a written warranty from the vendor that the horse is free from vice; some vets may ask as part of their building up of an overall picture, though they are not obliged to. There is nothing to stop you asking your vet to get an assurance from the vendor that the horse has no stable vices; if the animal starts weaving as soon as you get him home, you at least have a witness.

Height is another area that is not covered as part of the examination, though the vet will note an approximation. If you are buying a show horse where this is a vital concern—for instance, a cob that must not exceed 15.1hh without shoes—then you need an official height certificate obtained through the Joint Measurement Scheme. Animals up to the age of six are issued with annual certificates and at seven can be given one for life: if you buy a youngster you take the risk that he may go over height as he matures.

When you arrange the vetting, make sure your vet knows exactly what job the horse will be expected to do, and be realistic about it. If you are buying the horse to hack and compete in riding club competitions, do not let your dreams take over and tell the vet that you hope to be riding round Badminton Horse Trials in two years' time. A minor defect that would be of no consequence to the riding club horse could well be of much greater significance to the advanced event horse, so be fair to everyone including yourself.

It is up to you and your vet whether you are there when the examination is made. Some people like to go along, but many vendors, especially dealers, believe the vet should be left to do the job without interruption. Many vets feel the same way: it interrupts the examination procedure and their train of thought if they feel they have to keep breaking off to explain points.

The other point of view is, of course, that anyone who does not want the purchaser there when the horse is vetted has something to hide. It all comes down to personal choice, but if you do want to be there, keep quiet and let the vet get on with it. A good compromise can be to arrive at the end of the examination, when the vet has finished and is able to discuss his findings with you. If you cannot or do not want to be there, he will discuss the horse with you later.

Whatever the type of horse and whatever purpose he is intended for, the veterinary examination will be a methodical process divided into five distinct stages: the preliminary examination, trotting up, strenuous exercise, a period of rest and the second trot up and foot examination. Every vet will have his own way of doing things, but will work within this frame.

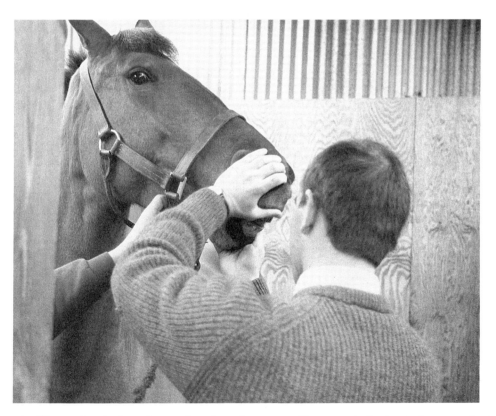

The vet will examine the horse's mouth and teeth to assess his age and whether he has any physical problems.

If you are buying an unbroken horse, it may be impossible for the vet to carry out the strenuous exercise part of the examination. However, it is still well worth having the horse vetted: problems such as eye and heart defects will be shown up and the vet can point out any conformation defects that might cause problems later on.

Preliminary examination

The first stage of the examination is usually carried out in the stable and enables the vet to form an overall impression of the horse and build a base with which to compare later findings. He will take in the horse's overall appearance and condition and go over him literally from head to tail.

He will look at the horse's teeth to get an approximation of age and examine the eyes with an ophthalmoscope, an instrument that helps detect signs of sight defects. At this stage the vet will also use a stethoscope to evaluate the animal's heart and lungs at rest; later this will compare with the same procedure carried out after the horse has been exercised.

The vet will ask to see the horse trotted up on a level surface.

As you have already done, he will run his hands over the animal's body and limbs to find defects such as splints, scars or abnormalities. The horse will be turned right round, the feet picked up and examined and the limbs flexed to see if there is any limitation of movement or signs of pain.

Once all this is done, the vet will ask for the horse to be taken outside in order to have a good look at him in daylight and if necessary—perhaps because visibility in the box was not good enough—repeat any of the procedures. If he finds that the animal is not fit to be exerted for the later stage of the procedure, for instance because he discovers a heart defect, the vetting will end because there is no point in going on.

Trotting up

This enables the vet to assess the horse's movement and, of course, to check for soundness. He will ask to see the horse led out on a headcollar, with the leadrope long enough to allow freedom of head and neck and to show the natural paces. Ideally, this part of the examination should be carried out on hard, level ground.

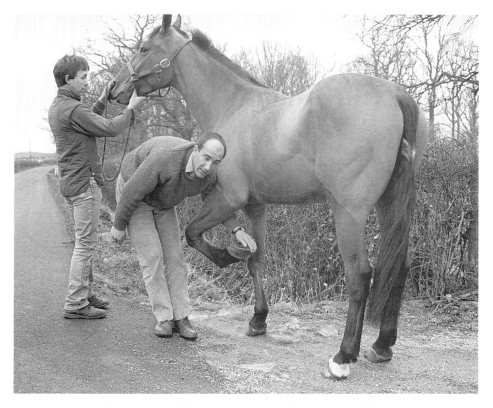

Flexion tests help to show up any lameness problems.

The horse will be walked about twenty yards away from the vet, turned round and walked back towards him. This will then be repeated at trot, though over about twice the distance to enable the vet to gauge the faster pace. The trot is the most important pace as far as the vetting is concerned, as it is here that signs of lameness are likely to show up. Usually only severe lameness shows at walk.

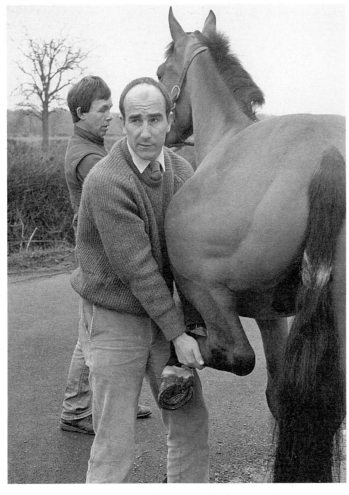

Flexion tests are done on all four limbs. They are not conclusive, but offer a guideline to an experienced vet.

If there is a problem at this stage because the animal appears to be unsound, the vet will stop his examination. Sometimes there is an obvious reason for a temporary lameness, such as an injury; if the seller can suggest a reasonable cause the vet may say it will be worth him coming back when the horse seems to have recovered. All you can do is take his advice and try not to be annoyed that the seller either did not notice the injury or hoped it would not make any difference.

Flexion tests are an area where different vets have different opinions, but most will carry them out. Each leg in turn is flexed and held for between forty-five seconds and a minute, and as soon as the vet releases his hold the horse is trotted up. It is not unusual for a horse to take a couple of lame or 'iffy' strides to start with (imagine how you would feel if someone held your leg bent double for a minute) but prolonged lameness is a danger sign. A low flexion test can reveal indications of problems such as navicular.

This sort of grey area emphasises the need for an experienced horse vet. One who has watched probably thousands of sound and lame horses moving will know when to be suspicious of a problem. Likewise, in some circumstances a vet may ask for a horse to be trotted in a circle on a hard surface; this again needs expert assessment, as the horse is moving in an unnatural way and a young or unschooled horse will put his head and neck to the outside to balance himself. This may result in shortened strides, and it takes an expert eye to work out the difference between lack of balance and lameness.

Strenuous exercise

The next part of the vetting is designed to find out if the horse has any defects that are only apparent after exerting himself. The vet will have already evaluated the animal's heart and lungs at rest, and now wants to see what they are like after stress.

The vet will listen to the horse's lungs and heart both at rest and after exercise.

If the horse is too young to be ridden it can be lunged, but the vet will expect any animal that is broken-in to be ridden. It is up to the vendor to either ride the horse or provide someone to ride it.

The vet wants to exert the horse, not exhaust it, and he will take its age, condition and fitness into account: for instance, a point-to-point horse in training will take more than an overweight, unfit cob. The horse will be cantered for between five and ten minutes, either in a school or in a field, and the vet will ask the rider to pass him on each circuit so that he can hear its breathing.

He will then ask the rider to move up a gear into a controlled gallop, and when he is satisfied that the horse has been exerted enough he will employ his stethoscope again on the heart and lungs. Facilities vary, but everyone selling a horse should have somewhere to canter and gallop.

Period of rest

The horse, who by now has worked pretty hard, will be put back in his stable and left to stand quietly for about half-an-hour. The vet will use this time to write up his notes, detailing the name, breeding or type, colour, markings, sex and age of the horse and any conditions of disease or injury that he has noticed so far. It is also a good opportunity to enjoy a cup of coffee!

The vet will want to see that the horse can turn a tight circle and cross his hind legs.

Second trot-up and foot examination

If you have got this far you at least have the consolation of knowing that you are on the home run. The horse will be brought up and walked and trotted in hand again, exactly as before. The vet will next want to see him turned sharply in his own length on both reins and backed up a few paces. A horse that cannot cross his hind legs when he turns or who backs up reluctantly (or not at all) may have a problem in the hind leg area.

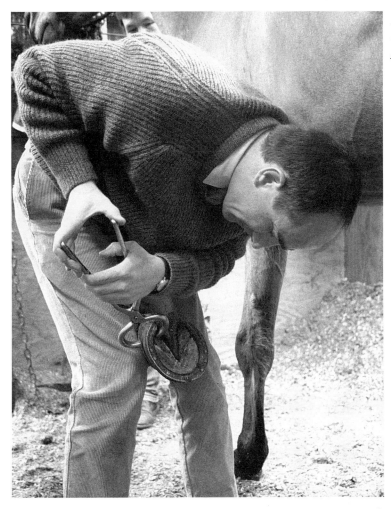

Hoof pincers are used to check if there are any painful areas.

The vet will examine the horse's feet, using pincers to test for sensitive areas. If he is worried about anything he may ask the seller's permission to remove a shoe or shoes; getting them put back on should remain the seller's responsibility unless the examination proceeds satisfactorily. You may then find yourself the proud owner of a new horse in desperate need of shoeing.

During this final stage the vet will check that the horse's heart and breathing rates have returned to normal, using his first readings as a base to work from.

Optional extras

There are other procedures that you may wish the vet to carry out. Taking blood samples is one of them and is always a good idea. It protects both you and the seller: if the horse goes lame four days after you get him home, you can at least find out whether he was on painkilling medication when he was vetted. Many dealers insist that vets always take blood samples from the horses they are selling.

There are two ways of dealing with blood samples. Some vets store them for between ten days and a month and only analyse them if, say, signs of lameness show up within that time, whilst other analyse them as standard. The first method is cheaper, but the second can be more useful in that it shows up whether, for instance, the horse is recovering from a virus or heavy worm infestation. From an insurance point of view, having the analysis done means that if the horse goes lame a day after the sample is thrown away, it can be proved that he was not on medication when you bought him.

Sometimes, especially if the horse is a very expensive one, the vet will recommend X-raying its feet and hocks. He may also want to do this if the horse seems sound but has a conformation problem that worries him, such as mismatched or boxy feet or poor hocks. In the case of an expensive, specialised show jumper or eventer it can be a wise precaution to make sure that the feet and hocks are likely to stand up to the strain they will be, or have already been, put under; again, it takes an expert to interpret X-rays and to decide what is significant and what can be disregarded.

If the vet thinks the horse has a wind problem, he may suggest endoscoping it to identify the cause. This enables him to look at the horse's respiratory tract; some practices have sophisticated endoscopes that link to video equipment enabling the horse's respiratory system to be seen on camera.

When the examination is over, the vet will discuss his findings with you. Again, this is where you want a good horse vet who can explain the pros and cons to you in plain English. Hopefully he will be able to recommend that you purchase the horse; he will point out any defects that he has found and tell you why, in his opinion, they will not affect the horse for your purpose.

If there is a problem that he thinks is temporary, such as an overreach or bruised foot that is causing mild lameness, the vet may well tell you that a repeat visit could be useful in a little while. It is then up to you to decide if you want to go through the procedure again; if you liked the horse enough to want to buy him in the first place, he should be worth another chance.

The worst scenario is when you really like the horse and the vet cannot recommend you to buy him. Remember that although his job is to tell you what is wrong with the horse, he bases his opinion on clinical judgement rather than personal prejudices: he will not turn down a horse just because he does not like chestnut mares. No matter how much you fell in love with the horse, it is sheer stupidity to go against the vet's recommendation; what is the point of paying for an expert's opinion and then ignoring it? Tell yourself that this one was not meant to be and carry on looking.

Hopefully the vet will tell you that he thinks the horse will be suitable for the job you want him to do. He will explain his findings and why they led him to that conclusion: for instance, the horse might have a splint, but it is not in a position to interfere with his movement and will not detract from his usefulness as a hunter. He will send you a written report that is a helpful description of your horse, as it includes all his natural and acquired markings, and will also detail information from the examination.

As soon as you have discussed the examination with the vet and he has recommended purchase it is your responsibility to pay for the horse and collect him. If you attend the vetting, you should take the cheque or cash with you and hand it over that day in return for a written receipt.

Most people will happily keep a horse for a few days if you are working and need to wait until the weekend or have to arrange transport, but do not expect to leave it any longer unless you have a good reason and are prepared to pay livery for the horse's keep.

Insurance

For the one or two horse owner, insurance is common sense rather than a luxury and it is something you should arrange as soon as the horse legally becomes yours. If you sort out the arrangements beforehand, you can literally make a phone call before you leave the vendor's yard and arrange immediate cover.

If you are buying a horse to replace one that was already insured, and the policy has not expired, it should be a simple matter of changing cover from one animal to the other. You will need to fill in another proposal form and may wish to change the cover you take out or the sum insured, particularly if your new horse is more valuable and you will be doing more with him than the previous one.

If this is your first horse, do some shopping around beforehand to get an idea of what the various companies offer and which you feel comfortable dealing with. In many ways, you can only tell how good an insurance company or broker is when there is a problem; whilst you hope this will not happen, look on the payment of your premium as peace of mind.

One way of finding out which insurance companies have a good reputation is to ask your vet and other horse owners. Vets are not allowed to act as agents for individual companies, but they will know from their own and their clients' experiences which ones are straightforward to deal with and pay claims promptly and which tend to make life more complicated.

A little research will probably result in the same names cropping up frequently. Give these companies a ring, explain that you are about to buy a horse and ask their advice about which sort of cover might be applicable. You can also ask for some specimen policies, which are essential but unfortunately not exactly light reading.

You will soon be able to tell if the person on the other end of the phone talks your language. The best insurance companies only employ people who own or have owned horses, to ensure that they understand what is involved and all the issues concerned. If you get the distinct impression that the person you are talking to does not know one end of a horse from the other, be careful about placing your business here: if you are not on the same wavelength when making initial inquiries, how much more difficult would it be if you were ringing up because your horse had a problem?

There are various types of insurance cover available, and you can choose between blanket policies or those that allow you to pick the cover you need. In most cases, the latter is preferable—there is no point, for instance, in paying for insurance on your tack if you keep it at home and it is covered on your household contents policy. (Do not, by the way, assume that this will be so: check!)

The most basic cover is for death of the horse, theft or straying. Obviously no one wants to think about their horse dying, but accidents happen. As with all insurance issues, you need to be aware of not only what is covered, but also what is not.

For instance, if a veterinary surgeon says that the animal is in such suffering that it must be destroyed, your insurance company will pay out: as always, either the sum insured or the market value, whatever is the less. There is rarely any argument over which applies, and you could argue that if the insurance company accepted your valuation when you paid your premium it also accepted that this was the horse's value—but that does not mean that you should insure a £500 pony for £3,000 just in case.

You will not be covered if you decide to have the horse put down for economic or other reasons. For instance, if a horse is injured in a way that means he cannot be ridden, but would be theoretically happy in retirement in a field, your insurance company will be unlikely to pay out.

For most owners, insurance against vets' fees is the main reason for taking out a policy. There have been incredible advances in veterinary science over the past few years, with the result that many conditions that might once have been incurable can now be treated, allowing the horse to return to a useful life. Research into drugs and the use of sophisticated diagnostic techniques do not come cheap, so veterinary bills can be quite terrifying.

For instance, if a horse suffers an attack of colic and it is thought that only surgery might save him, you could well end up with a bill of more than £2,000 and it will be the same whether the patient is a £300 pony or a £30,000 top competition horse. Scanning, X-rays and other diagnostic techniques are also expensive.

If you have the right veterinary fees cover, you can do the best for your horse whatever happens. It does not guarantee that he can be saved or even returned to a working life, but he will have the best chance. Think how terrible it must be to tell a vet to destroy an animal that might recover because you could not pay the bill at the end of it.

As always, you need to check what different companies offer for their veterinary fee cover. It varies tremendously, and the cheapest policy may not necessarily give you the best cover if things go wrong.

For a start, is the amount of cover fixed at a standard maximum sum or is it linked to the value of the horse and sum insured? To return to our colic scenario, the bill will be the same no matter what the value of the horse. If you are only covered up to your £300 pony's value, you will be left with £1700 to find.

Is the maximum cover high enough? With vets' fees increasing all the time, you need a minimum of £2,000 per incident and some companies are offering £3,000. You also need to check whether you will be covered for an enormous bill and any further problems. Some policies state, for instance, that cover is a maximum £2,000 per incident and unlimited in total, whereas others state it is a maximum £2,000 per incident and £2,000 in total.

Skills such as physiotherapy and remedial shoeing can be enormously valuable in getting a horse back in action, but they too can leave you with a hefty bill. Eight physiotherapy sessions at £30 per time work out at rather more than loose change and if complementary treatment is not included in your cover, it will be down to you to pay.

Some policies include complementary treatment as part of the standard cover, whilst others make it an optional extra. If you have ever needed to pay for it, you will appreciate that shaving £15 or so off your premium might turn out to be false economy.

In equine medicine, as in the human kind, there are unfortunately practitioners whose pedigree is, to put it charitably, doubtful. For this reason, insurance companies inevitably specify that anyone carrying out complementary treatment on your horse must do so with the permission and under the supervision of your vet.

If your horse has a problem that necessitates you claiming vets' fees, the insurance company may impose an exclusion when your policy is renewed. For instance, if he develops a sarcoid, you may find that when your policy comes up for renewal the insurers will not pay out any further claims relating to warts, sarcoids or tumours. It may seem unfair from your point of view, but their reasoning is that problems are likely to recur—it is a bit like losing your no claims bonus on your car insurance, though rather more drastic.

A lot of people lose out because they do not realise that they can ask their insurers to reconsider if they believe the exclusion is unfair. The usual procedure is that you will be asked to provide a letter from your vet stating that in their opinion, the condition is not likely to arise again. If the insurance company refuses to lift or amend the exclusion, you have two options: accept it or insure elsewhere.

Bear in mind that insurance companies ask you to disclose any previous problems so you might find the same exclusion being imposed. If you are tempted to forget about the problem remember that if the insurers find out, your insurance will be invalid. If the condition does arise again, your vet will have to disclose that he has treated the animal for the same condition in the past.

The other thing you need to consider is whether or not to take out insurance for permanent incapacity, commonly known as loss of use. Although this is the most expensive form of cover, it may be one you want to consider if you are paying a lot of money for a competition horse.

It is important to understand what loss of use means. A lot of people misinterpret it, and it leads to more confusion and controversy than any other form of insurance cover. The key factor is that it will only be agreed if the horse is permanently incapable of doing the job for which it is insured; if there is a chance that he will be able to return to work after treatment and/or a rest period, you will have to wait and see what the outcome is.

The usual rule of thumb is that if the horse is still unable to do the job a year after the claim was submitted, it will be agreed. In clear-cut cases, some companies will take the opinion of your veterinary surgeon alone whilst others want a second opinion as a matter of routine.

If loss of use is agreed, the company will agree a residual value with you and pay the sum insured (or market value) minus that amount. For instance, if a horse is insured for show jumping, dressage and hacking and has an accident leaving him permanently incapable of doing anything but hacking, your insurance company will negotiate a value for him based on that limited ability and pay you the difference between the two.

Check whether you will be paid the full sum insured or a percentage of it; some companies pay out 100 per cent but others only 75 per cent. Alternatively, your company may offer 75 per cent as standard but 100 per cent if you opt for higher premiums.

It is up to you to do your own sums and work out whether loss of use cover is an investment or something you can do without. Few people take it up on horses worth £2,000 or less.

Chapter 10
Equipment

Buying a horse sometimes seems like endless expense, especially if you have to purchase all his tack, rugs and equipment from scratch. Flick through any saddler's catalogue and you will get an idea of what the well-dressed horse is wearing; indulgent owners with bottomless bank balances can buy whole wardrobes of rugs, bandages and what have you, but most of us have to work to a more realistic budget. Start with the essentials and leave the trimmings for later—a wool day rug with your initials or sponsor's name in the corner is part of the professional's image-boosting package, but is not essential for the average amateur.

Whatever you buy, whether it is tack, rugs or stable equipment, go for the best quality you can afford. In the long run you will get more for your money; cheap equipment tends to be badly designed and less hard wearing. A cheap and cheerful New Zealand, for instance, will probably not be shaped round the shoulders and quarters and will be more likely to rub.

You may be offered the chance to buy your horse or pony's tack and rugs with him. If they are good quality and fit well, this can be a useful bargaining point. If you are not sure about either point, get expert advice. (*Tack: How to Choose it and Use it*, by Carolyn Henderson, also published by Swan Hill Press, gives a thorough insight.)

Tack

Good quality, well-fitting tack is essential. It might sound obvious, but at any competition there are horses with bits that are the wrong size, nosebands that are incorrectly adjusted and saddles that pinch or rub. If a horse is uncomfortable, he will not work properly; after all, imagine how you would feel if you were asked to work in shoes that were too tight or too big.

Discomfort affects your powers of concentration, whether you are a horse or a human, and can also make you irritable and bad tempered. The tack also needs to fit you, so beware of stirrup irons that are too small and saddle flaps that are too short and catch on the top of your boots.

If you have to buy tack elsewhere and are on a limited budget, buying good quality secondhand will often give you better value than new tack that is of a poorer standard. If you find it hard to judge new leather, look at the finish: finishing touches take time and time means money. No one is going to spend hours hand-stitching a bridle from cheap leather because they will not be able to charge a price that reflects the work involved.

Most tack today is machine-stitched, and there is nothing wrong with that. It is simple economics: a machine-stitched bridle costs a third of the price of a hand-stitched one. But in both cases, make sure that the leather and stitching are in a good state of repair. Check all the parts where metal rests on leather, for instance where the stirrup leathers bear the weight of the irons and the reins fasten on to the bit.

Stitching is another common area of weakness, so give a good pull at leathers, reins, and anything that looks vulnerable—get hold of the two parts stitched together and give a hard tug. It might be embarrassing if it comes apart in your hands, but think how much worse it would be if it happened while you were riding. Everything should appear workmanlike: flimsy bootlace bridles with shoestring reins do not flatter any horse, no matter how finely made he is, and will not take the strain.

Bits and bridles

In general it is sensible to keep to the bit and noseband that the horse is used to. It might be tempting to wonder how he would go in, say, a different kind of snaffle or a drop noseband instead of a cavesson, but if you were happy enough with the way he went when you tried him, why alter things unless, when you get to know him, you feel that a change in tack could help to achieve a specific aim?

Whatever bit you start with, make sure it is the right size for the horse's mouth. Many people use bits that are too big, so that the mouthpiece pulls through from one side to the other and the joint or joints are off-centre. A bit that is too big drops down too far in the horse's mouth, which can encourage him to put his tongue over it.

Conversely, one that is too small will pinch or rub, especially if it has loose rings. You should aim for a bit that allows a quarter of an inch each side between the rings and the horse's lips and it should be high enough to wrinkle the corners of the lips slightly.

The commonest types of snaffle are the single-jointed, half-moon or straight bar, and double-jointed. All can have various cheekpieces that affect their action—a loose ring affords more play, an eggbutt or D-ring helps keep the bit still and full cheeks are a great help with steering a green or ignorant horse. It is often said that the thicker the mouthpiece, the kinder the action, but this is not always true.

A horse with a shallow mouth or a thick tongue may find a thick, single-jointed snaffle uncomfortable because it puts too much pressure on his tongue. He will probably be happier with a French link snaffle (not to be confused with the more severe Dr Bristol, which has a flat-sided centre plate) or a thinner, tapered snaffle. Some horses resent the nutcracker action of a single-jointed snaffle and are happier with a French link or half-moon mouthpiece.

The bridle should be the correct weight for the horse's head. But while a Thoroughbred will look best in a lighter bridle rather than that which suits a heavyweight cob, it should still have some substance to it. It should also be adjusted carefully: common mistakes are browbands that pinch the ears and nosebands that are too low. Flash nosebands that are too lightweight are the worst: as soon as the drop strap is fastened the cavesson part is dragged down. A decent weight of leather, fastened securely but not too tightly, will prevent this.

A cavesson noseband should be fitted so it does not rub the cheekbones. The textbook rule is to fit two fingers' width between the back fastening and the horse's head, but you can tighten it a hole if necessary. A drop noseband should be fitted so that the top part lays on the bony part of the nose (if it rests on the soft part it is too low and can interfere with the horse's breathing) and again two fingers should be able to slip between the back part and the curb groove.

A beautifully made bridle like this one, which complements the horse's type, would be well worth buying.

A flash noseband should have the top part fastened snugly but not too tightly, and there should be room for at least a finger between the bottom strap and the horse's jaw. Grakle nosebands should have the crossover point on the centre of the horse's nose and again, there should be space to get a finger between the straps and face. The idea of any form of dropped noseband is to prevent the horse from opening his mouth too wide, not to clamp it shut so tightly that he cannot flex his jaw.

If your horse goes in a pelham some of the time, it should be fitted so that it is snug up into the corners of the mouth without wrinkling them. The curb chain should lie flat in the chin groove and should come into play when the curb cheeks are drawn back to an angle of 45 degrees.

The commonest form of pelham is the mullen-mouthed or half-moon one, with a mouthpiece of either vulcanite (hardened rubber) or metal. Specialists, especially producers of show horses, use lots of other kinds. The Hanoverian pelham has a roller incorporated into the mouthpiece to encourage the horse to mouth, and the SM pelham (named after its inventor, Sam Marsh) has a broad, flat mouthpiece that is hinged at each side to give independent rein action.

Headcollars

A leather headcollar is essential for travelling, though a washable nylon one is fine for everyday use. Horses should never be turned out in nylon headcollars because they may not break if they get caught up on something (whereas the horse's neck might). When buying a secondhand one, check the stitching and the areas where metal fittings rest on leather.

Saddles

Most people use a general purpose saddle, unless they specialise to the extent that a dressage or jumping model is needed. Whatever the cut, it must fit as well as possible—a badly fitting saddle can do a lot of damage to a horse's back. A good secondhand saddle or even one of the new synthetics can be a better buy than a new but poor quality leather one.

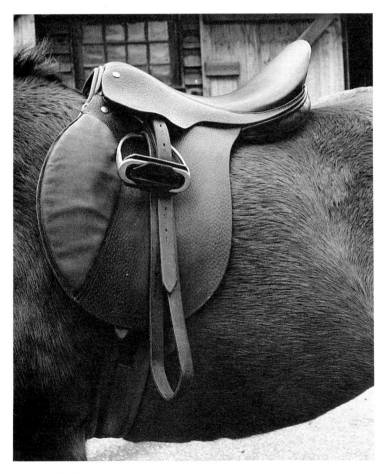

You may be offered the chance to buy your horse's tack with him. A well-fitting saddle in good condition, like this one, could also be a good buy.

If you are offered the horse's present saddle, check it carefully for signs of damage and wear. Start with the tree (the framework it is built on). Place it on a flat surface, put your hands on either side of the front arch, press hard and hope that you do not hear peculiar creaks or grinding noises. A spring tree saddle will have a certain amount of give, but there should be no excessive movement.

Next hold the saddle with the pommel against your stomach, seat towards you. Take hold of the cantle and pull hard again, you should not get excessive movement or strange noises. Either can be a signal that the saddle has been damaged, usually in a fall or because someone dropped it. If you have any doubts, ask to have it checked over by a good saddler.

When you look at the saddle on the horse's back it should seem to belong there, not be perched on top. The best designs have a wide bearing surface that spreads the weight of the rider evenly over the horse's back, and a gullet that is wide enough to prevent pressure on the spine. A saddle should not interfere with the movement of the horse's shoulder.

When you are mounted the saddle should stay comfortably in place without rocking. Anyone standing behind should be able to see a channel of daylight through to the pommel, and there should be adequate clearance between the pommel and the wither. The textbook guideline is three fingers' width, but slightly less may be acceptable in some cases—again get a good saddle-fitter's advice.

Horses with high or low withers, straight or loaded shoulders and other conformation faults are much more difficult to fit than ones with a generally good make and shape, and you will need an expert saddle-fitter to help you. Not all people who make and sell saddles qualify on that count, so find someone with a good reputation. The Society of Master Saddlers now runs in-depth saddle-fitting courses for its members, so anyone who has gained a qualification on one of these should be well competent.

If your new horse's tack is not for sale and you have a limited amount to spend, you have two options—a secondhand leather saddle or a new synthetic one. The most reliable way of buying secondhand is through a good saddler, who may have a suitable saddle taken in part exchange against another.

The advantage is that he will already have checked it over and made any necessary minor repairs, and he may be able to fit it for you and make any adjustments to the flocking that are needed. Secondhand saddles are often advertised for sale in horse magazines and you may get a perfectly good buy as long as you know what you are looking for and follow the same provisos on fitting.

Most horse sales and auctions have a section for tack and equipment, but again, they present a big risk for the amateur buyer. There used to be a lot of tack offered through these made from poor quality leather, often Indian; it looked nice enough to the uneducated eye, but would not stand up to sufficient strain. Fortunately there is not so much of it about now, though you will see a lot of worn or damaged English tack that is just as dangerous.

Synthetic saddles are frowned upon by traditionalists, and a synthetic will never have the aesthetic appeal of a good leather one. Even so, the better makes are light, hard-wearing and easy to look after. If you hate cleaning tack, a washable synthetic that can be hosed down might appeal! They are usually about half the price of leather saddles.

This synthetic saddle is well-made, but does not fit this horse. It would only be worth buying if an experienced saddle-fitter could adjust it.

Do not make the mistake of thinking that because a saddle is lightweight, it cannot hurt the horse. A badly fitting synthetic saddle that causes pressure points can do just as much damage as any other, so pay as much attention to fitting (and who fits it!) as with a leather one.

Stirrup leathers should be made from strong, good quality leather and the stitching should be checked regularly for wear. Some of the manufacturers of synthetic saddles offer synthetic leathers to go with them, and claim that their materials are stronger and more hard-wearing than leather. The drawbacks are that the holes tend to stretch, and some synthetics can rub if used with leather saddles.

Stirrup irons *must* be the correct size for the rider; far too many people use ones that are too small and risk getting their foot trapped. There should be a half inch space on each side of the widest part of the foot, and the arch must be high enough to allow you to slip your feet out of the irons easily.

Most people like to use a numnah underneath the saddle; it keeps it clean and if you use one made from natural fibre it will absorb sweat. Avoid numnahs made from synthetic fabrics because they can set up irritation. When you put the saddle on, make sure the numnah is pulled up into the arch to prevent pressure.

A numnah cannot compensate for a badly fitting saddle, so do not assume that an extra thick one will prevent damage. In fact, if the saddle fits correctly a numnah that is too thick can cause problems; it is rather like wearing two pairs of socks inside a pair of shoes that were the right size to start with.

Nothing looks nicer than a good quality leather girth, which must be kept clean and supple, but they are expensive. For everyday use many people like the padded fabric ones that are supposed to absorb sweat, but they must be washed regularly.

Girths are measured in increments of two inches, from buckle end to buckle end. The perfect size is one that does not need to be buckled higher than the third or fourth hole on either side, so there is no unwanted bulk under the rider's legs.

Martingales and breastplates

Martingales are auxiliary aids that, in theory, no well-schooled horse should need, although there are times when it is sensible to use one. Bear in mind that their purpose is to stop the horse's head going above the point of control, *not* to strap it down.

The standing martingale, which goes from the girth to a cavesson noseband, passes in and out of fashion. It used to be standard equipment in the hunting field and is still used by many hunting people. The advantage of a standing martingale is that it does not interfere with the bit and as such it can be a short-term safety measure on a young or unschooled horse that throws its head up. The disadvantage is that a horse can learn to lean against it, building up muscle exactly where you do not want it on the underside of the neck.

The standard fitting allows the martingale to be pushed into the horse's gullet, but it may need to be slightly shorter to be effective. It should always be used with a rubber stop at the junction of the strap that goes from noseband to girth and the neckstrap. This prevents it dangling between the horse's front legs and getting caught.

A standing martingale should only be fastened to a cavesson noseband; if you need some kind of drop action as well then you should use a flash (with the martingale fastened to the cavesson strap) and start schooling your horse!

The running martingale starts from the girth and splits into two straps with a ring at each end, through which the reins pass. It is designed to keep the bit on the bars of the horse's mouth, thus affording greater control, but it needs careful fitting to make sure it does not interfere. A bib martingale is a variation on the running variety where the straps are joined together with a triangular piece of leather. It is used on horses who have learned the endearing habit of catching hold of the straps in their teeth and has a definite limiting action on the reins.

Both these martingales should be used with a rubber stop at the neckstrap junction, as with the standing. It is also important to use rubber stops on the reins to prevent the rings catching on the rein buckles or billets.

Breastplates and breastgirths are used for extra security and to help keep the saddle in place. A well-shaped horse with a well-fitting saddle should not need either, except as a safety measure when jumping big fences cross-country (which is why many event riders use one, plus an over-girth). However, a horse that tends to be flat-sided or herring-gutted, or one with especially high withers, may need the extra help this piece of tack can offer.

A hunting breastplate attaches to the girth and then to the front D-rings of the saddle via two short straps on either side of the withers. Neither the breastplate nor its neckstrap should be too tight, and you can buy martingale attachments if necessary.

A breastgirth is often seen on racehorses, though they have also become popular with show jumpers, and comprises a band of elastic or webbing that goes across the horse's chest and fastens to the girth on each side. A strap over the withers keeps it in the right position. The drawback is that if the fit is anything less than perfect it can press on the horse's windpipe and affect his breathing.

Boots and bandages

Some people use leg protection such as brushing boots as a matter of course, while others believe they are only necessary for jumping or to prevent a young, unbalanced horse or a bad mover knocking himself. Certainly they can be a wise precaution when starting riding your new horse because he will be unsure of himself and more likely to knock himself.

The commonest brushing boots are the washable kind with Velcro fastenings, while at the top end of the market you can buy leather boots with strap and buckle fastenings and even ones made from special high-density plastic that moulds to the horse's leg. A lot of the really cheap boots are not worth buying because they simply do not offer enough protection.

Other boots in common use are overreach and tendon styles. Overreaches can be nasty injuries that are slow and difficult to heal, so again boots are a wise precaution at first, and many people use them as standard when jumping. The traditional design is a rubber bell that either pulls over the foot or fastens with Velcro; be careful that they are not too long, so that the horse treads on the bottom and trips himself up. This cannot happen with the newer petal variety, where replaceable petals simply pull out from a retaining band.

Tendon boots are the show jumpers' favourites, and many event riders like to use them for fast work; if a horse strikes into a tendon at speed he can do an awful lot of damage. They protect the vulnerable tendon area but are usually open at the front, so if a show jumper raps a pole with his forelegs he is likely to feel it and (in theory) snap up sharper next time.

Horses' legs should always be protected whilst travelling (see Chapter 11) unless you are transporting a young unbroken horse that has never worn anything before and is likely to be upset by strange things suddenly being wrapped round his legs. For an older animal you can choose between travelling bandages over Gamgee or similar padding or specially designed boots; the latter are easier to put on, but many people prefer bandages for long journeys as they are less likely to slip.

Rugs

Rugs are expensive, so if your horse's wardrobe is in good condition and you are offered it at a reasonable price, take advantage of the fact. If you are buying new ones, start with the basics of two New Zealands and a stable rug; extras like summer sheets and sweat rugs can come later. You need two New Zealands so that if one gets soaked through or damaged, you have a spare whilst it is being dried or repaired.

A beautifully cut rug that can be worn indoors and out. This design is a Rambo rug by Horseware.

The most expensive will be no good if they do not fit your horse, so measure him from the centre of his chest to the end of his quarters to get the length needed. Rugs usually come in three inch increments from four foot nine inches to six foot nine inches; it takes a big horse to fill a six foot nine rug. Do not buy an extra large rug because you think it will cover more of him and keep him warmer – all that will happen is that it will slip and rub.

The problem with rugs is that horses, like people, do not come in standard sizes. A well-made animal will be easy to kit out, but conformation problems such as very high withers or straight shoulders will affect the fit of a rug. Some market research can pay off, so ask friends with horses of similar type to yours what make of rugs they bought and what advantages and drawbacks they have found.

There are some designs that seem a good fit on almost any type of horse as long as you buy the right size to start with. They all have design points in common, especially the way they are cut high on the neck. If a rug is too low in the neck it will slip back and cause rubs.

There are so many designs of New Zealand on the market that it is often difficult to see the wood for the trees. Basically you have a choice between natural fibres, like flax, and synthetics, like the new breathable fabrics. The good synthetics can be unbeatable because they are lightweight and as waterproof as you can hope for.

Do be realistic when buying rugs. No rug can be totally waterproof because a small amount of water is bound to seep through fastenings and stitch holes, though many do an excellent job. Nor can any rug stand up to a horse's teeth, though any retailer will tell you that some people do expect this. Buyers also complain when, for instance, legstraps break, forgetting that a rug must have a breaking point if it is to be safe. If your horse gets caught up somewhere, which would you rather broke—his legstrap or his leg?

It is important to differentiate between a heavy duty New Zealand and a lightweight turnout rug. The latter is designed to be worn when a horse is turned out for a couple of hours a day, so you cannot expect it to be as effective as a New Zealand.

A good New Zealand will stay in place when the horse rolls, and there are a variety of fastenings. The commonest are leg straps and cross-surcingles, but there are also some very good spider pattern systems that look confusing but are, in fact, easy to manage; a network of fastening straps radiates out from a central point and fastens to linking points down the sides of the rug.

Washable, lightweight stable rugs with cotton linings have all but replaced the old-fashioned jute type. They usually have cross surcingles, which should be stitched on in such a way that the strain is taken over a wide area to avoid the risk of a ripped rug. You can also buy rugs with spider pattern fastenings, which many people feel are best of all.

Cotton summer sheets and sweat rugs (sometimes called coolers) are useful but not immediately essential. A better bet is a lightweight, thermal rug made from special knitted fabric that wicks moisture away from the horse and through to the outer surface. These rugs are incredibly versatile and can be used in the stable, for travelling or for putting on a wet or sweating horse.

Yard, grooming and first aid equipment

If you are embarking on your horse-owning career, your spending is not yet over! Most livery yards will expect you to provide your own feed and water buckets, haynets and so on. Some yards provide mucking out tools, whilst others expect you to buy your own.

You will also need grooming and first aid kits, both of which can either be bought as complete kits or made up to your own requirements. Look at both options because complete packages can sometimes work out cheaper.

To muck out effectively you will need a fork, shovel, heavy duty broom and wheelbarrow. Some yards use traditional muck sacks, large canvas sheets with handles on which the muck and dirty bedding is piled before being folded up and carried to the heap. As they are heavy and not at all pleasant to handle, most people prefer wheelbarrows.

All your equipment needs to be the right size and weight for you to handle. Gardening forks are useless, as they are too heavy and the blunted prongs will not sift and lift bedding. Look for modern designs with lightweight handles, and if you intend to keep your horse on a shavings bed you may find a special shavings fork useful.

Some livery yards will expect you to provide your own mucking out tools.

Shavings users will find a pair of heavy duty rubber gloves essential. You have not joined the ranks of official horse owners until you have mastered the delights of donning rubber gloves to pick up dung piles—nowhere near as unpleasant as it sounds but a task that many men shirk from for some reason! They will also be useful for picking up piles from the paddock: much easier than trying to lift them with a shovel.

If you or your partner/helper have too much of a delicate nature to contemplate this task, you could invest in one of the special dung pickers. These comprise a container that looks like a giant dustpan with a short-handled rake and are, to all intents and purposes, the equestrian equivalent of the dog owner's poop scoop.

Shovels with heavy duty plastic heads are much easier to manage than traditional metal ones, and also last longer. Yard brooms should have stiff bristles and wide heads; ordinary ones are fine for sweeping stable floors, but if you have a big yard area to keep clean one of the extra wide brooms or an American style witches' broom is useful.

Wheelbarrows can range from ordinary garden ones to huge, purpose-built models for big yards. The best designs are well-balanced and unfortunately have large enough price tags to put them out of the range of most one-horse owners. Even if you can afford a big barrow, make sure you can push it fully loaded without straining yourself.

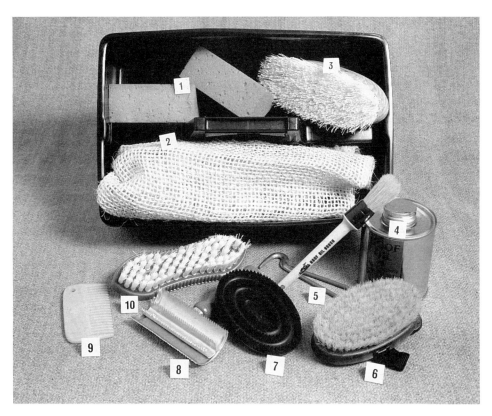

A useful grooming kit, comprising sponges, cactus stain removing cloth, dandy brush, hoof oil and brush, hoofpick, body brush, rubber and metal curry combs, mane comb and water brush.

Many horse owners suffer from bad backs; physiotherapists say it is not so much that riding causes back problems as that it shows up problems that are already there. However, that may seem small comfort when you are halfway through mucking out and your back feels as if you have already coped with a dozen dirty boxes. It is often far better to make two journeys with a small barrow that you can manage easily than one with a megabarrow that you can barely push.

If you have enough money left over to spend on useful things that do not count as essentials, invest in a rubber skep (pronounced skip: the horse world has a language of its own full of words that are spelt one way and pronounced another). This is useful for collecting the pile of dung that your horse deposits just as you are about to get on him, odd bits of rubbish and so on when you do not want to fetch a wheelbarrow.

There are several designs of feed buckets and mangers, ranging from portable mangers that slot into triangular-shaped frames in stable corners to shallow, wide diameter buckets designed to be set in the middle of an old tyre. The idea of the latter is that it stops the horse kicking an ordinary bucket over, but some can beat anything that equipment manufacturers come up with!

Indestructible feed buckets made from tough rubber defeat most horses' hooves and teeth, at least for a while. Hook-on mangers that fasten to a stable door can be useful for horses who take a mouthful of feed, rush to the door in case they are missing anything, then go back to their mangers.

Hay shortages have made more people aware of the value of forage feeds such as Dengie Hi-Fi, which is made from alfalfa and has a nutritional value equivalent to that of good quality hay. You need large containers because it is bulky; DIY stores have large plastic ones sold as log baskets or garden containers that do the job well.

If your stable does not have an automatic waterer, you will need one large or two smaller water buckets, enough to hold eight gallons at a time. Water buckets, like so many things such as grooming kit containers can be cheaper to buy from DIY and hardware stores than from specialist equestrian suppliers. In fairness, you must make sure that those from non-specialist shops are as robust.

Feeding hay in a haynet is less wasteful than feeding it loose.

When feeding hay, you have three options: it can either be fed on the ground, in a hayrack or in a haynet. Advocates of the first method say it is the most natural and the most conducive to building up the correct muscle structure. Horses eat naturally from the ground and it is a contradiction in terms to build up the muscles on the topline through schooling and encourage the building up of opposing ones underneath the neck by asking the horse to reach upwards for his hay.

This method is the most wasteful, though, because horses are great ones for trampling their hay into their beds. For this reason, most people opt for metal hayracks or haynets. Hayracks are more expensive to buy but cheaper on a cost per use basis, especially if you have the sort of horse who mauls his hay and rips his haynet to shreds in the process.

Chapter 11
Early Days

The first few weeks of your partnership with your new horse will be very much a getting to know each other process, when hopefully you will lay a good foundation for future progress. Be realistic in your expectations—professionals may buy a horse on Thursday and have it competing at a show on Saturday, but most people need to go rather more slowly.

On the other hand, you should not go so slowly that the horse gets out of the habit of working. A lot of people are so anxious to give a new horse time to settle down that they end up with problems when they decide to ride what is basically an over fresh horse.

If possible, arrange to collect the horse or have him delivered during the day so that he will have time to take in his new surroundings. It is not a disaster if this is impossible, but it does help to keep things relaxed.

You may be able to persuade the vendors to deliver the horse, particularly if they want to see him settle in. The advantages to this are obvious; the disadvantages are that you do not want to have to cope with tearful owners saying goodbye to their horse or pony and perhaps unsettling him. If you can trust them to be sensible, it is a convenient option.

Some dealers will include local delivery as part of the deal if they have someone available, but they tend to be the exception rather than the rule: delivering horses ties up someone who could be doing other things. However, if you do not have your own transport a dealer will usually know of a reliable professional transporter who will do the job for you.

It is important that whoever fetches the horse is experienced in both handling and driving skills. This is not the time to borrow a Land Rover and trailer and make your first attempt at towing!

If you are buying a youngster who has not travelled before, it is better to hire a good professional transporter who is used to dealing with youngstock. Ask local studs who they would recommend, as you want the horse's first experience of travelling to be as free from stress as possible.

The equipment needed to travel your horse will depend on his age and the time of year, but a leather headcollar is always essential. Nylon headcollars are dangerous for travelling for the same reason that they are unsafe for turning out—if the horse gets caught up, they might not break in time.

Most breeders travel youngstock without leg protection because they feel it is safer than the horse being worried by the unaccustomed feel of boots or bandages. The exception is if the horse's owners have already accustomed him to wearing them, but few people think that far ahead.

The mature horse will need either well-designed travelling boots or bandages and padding. Boots are quicker and easier to manage, but only a few designs can be relied on to stay in place without rubbing or slipping. The ones shown here are shaped to fit the horse's legs and the Velcro fastening straps are in the correct places; many cheap boots have little or no shaping and may slip down the horse's legs.

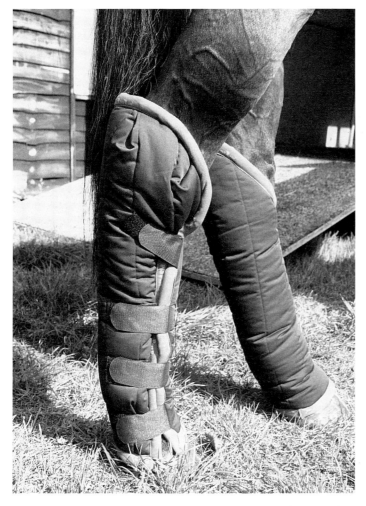

Travelling boots like these, which fit well and do not slip, are ideal for bringing your new horse home.

Most professionals prefer to use bandages for long journeys because if these are put on correctly they are less likely to slip than anything else. They must always be used over padding, either Fybagee or similar material or padded fabric leg quilts. The advantage of the latter is that bedding, especially shavings, does not stick to them.

Some people like to use knee and hock boots, but so many designs tend to slip. To keep them in place often requires the top straps to be fastened so tight that they end up doing more harm than good. If you are worried that your horse will be vulnerable, use shaped bandage pads that cover the knees and hocks.

You will need a tail bandage and/or tailguard to stop him rubbing the hair at the top of his tail and a pollguard is a wise precaution with a big horse or one who is known to throw his head about. If you use a pollguard with earholes, make sure they are big enough and if not, cut them larger. Horses hate having their ears pinched, and one who is uncomfortable or irritated will throw his head about more than ever.

A mature horse who is used to wearing rugs will need an appropriate one for travelling. This may range from a light cotton sheet in summer to a knitted thermal or other appropriate design in cold weather. Remember that vehicles need to be ventilated, and even in hot weather there will be a through-flow of air as you go along: your horse will not be able to move out of the way of any draughts, so it is important that he is protected from them.

On arriving home, take your horse into his stable so that you can remove his travelling gear and make sure that he is cool, comfortable and has not managed to bang or cut himself on the way. Check that he can see at least one other horse and is not the only one on the block; even the quietest animal will be worried if he thinks he is suddenly the only horse in the world.

If all is well, you may want to turn him out in the field to relax and have a roll. In an ideal world, a new arrival will go out for the first time in a small field with a companion who can be guaranteed to behave quietly, such as an old pony. Once he settles down, he can be introduced to a larger field with the horses who will be his usual companions.

In the real world, few yards can offer such luxury and he may have to go straight out with the others. There are always fewer squabbles if mares and geldings are kept in separate fields but even if this is the case, your horse will have to find his place in the pecking order.

Domestic horses maintain the herd hierarchy of their wild ancestors. There is always a dominant horse, one who is the most subservient and others in between. Your horse will find his place over the next few days, hopefully with nothing more than a few squeals and threatening expressions.

No matter how careful you are, turning out a new horse is always a case of crossing your fingers and hoping that flying hooves do not connect. Some people like to put brushing boots on as a precaution when they first turn horses out, but it is not a good idea to do this all the time. They are not designed to be worn for hours on end and dirt and sweat may collect underneath, causing rubs and sores.

At first, your new horse may be ostracised by the others. Do not feel too sorry for him if you see him grazing on the outskirts of the group, eventually one of the others will accept him, and gradually he will gain full membership. He may pair up with another horse or becomes everyone's friend: if you are unlucky, he could be the horse who causes all the trouble and is constantly being cursed by other owners!

Feeding

Find out what your new horse has been fed in his previous home before you work out his diet. A lot of people are vague in terms of quantities and will talk about a double handful of this or half a bucketful of that, but at least you will know whether his previous owners were feeding a low energy mix, high fibre cubes or whatever.

Even if you intend to change the type of feed, start off with what he is used to. Sudden changes in diet are one of the commonest causes of colic and stress is another, so bearing in mind that moving to a new home inevitably puts a horse under stress, you are asking for trouble if you add the two together.

Do not worry if he seems isolated from the crowd at first.

Also check what sort of hay or haylage he has been getting. Haylage, which is basically preserved forage grown specially for horses and packed in heat-sealed bags, has a higher feed value than most hays and as it is dust and virtually spore free, does not need to be soaked.

It is far better to err on the side of caution when feeding a new horse. Turn him out as much as possible, give him plenty of hay when necessary and keep concentrates to a minimum until you know him a bit better. His hard feed can always be increased as his work increases, but you do not want to have to ride or lunge him into the ground to work off excess energy.

Feeding causes a lot of confusion, but most of it can be avoided if you remember some basic principles on what and how much to feed. One of the most important foundations of any feeding plan is that horses are grazing animals: their digestive system is designed to take forage, not cereals.

The percentage of forage to hard feed should be at least 60:40 and will often be higher. In some cases, such as native ponies, good quality forage will be all they need and they will have to have their grazing limited when the grass is at its richest.

When we domesticate horses and ask them to work hard, forage cannot provide all the necessary fuel. To make up for that, we add hard feed, but good quality forage should still be the main part of the diet.

He will soon settle in—a good roll is a sign that he is starting to relax.

How much your horse needs to eat depends on his bodyweight, type, age and the amount and type of work he is doing. Work on the basis that he needs a daily total of 2.5 per cent of his bodyweight. There are three ways of calculating bodyweight: using a weighbridge, a weightape or a mathematical formula.

A weighbridge is the most accurate, though it is not always easy to find one. Weightapes, which have the girth measurement on one side and the horse's equivalent weight on the other, are a good rough guide but not always spot on in their accuracy.

The other method is to take two measurements and use a mathematical formula to calculate bodyweight. Measure the horse's length from the point of the shoulder to the point of the buttocks, and also the girth. Square the girth measurement and multiply it by the length, then divide the answer by 8717 to calculate the horse's weight in kilogrammes.

Traditionalists who prefer to work in inches and pounds should take the same two measurements. Again, square the girth measurement and multiply it by the length, working in inches. This time, divide the answer by 241 to give you the horse's weight in pounds.

Most feed bags give approximate bodyweights according to height, but these have to be very general. A 15hh Thoroughbred will weigh a lot less than a 15hh cob, and the difference in temperaments should also be taken into account. A laid-back horse or pony will usually be a much better doer than an excitable or nervous type.

You have the choice of feeding either straight cereals, oats or barley, or compound feeds formulated by feed companies in the form of either coarse mix or cubes. In 99 per cent of cases, compound feeds are by far the best choice as long as they are fed correctly.

The reason is that they have been formulated to include all the necessary vitamins, minerals and so on that your horse needs. The quality is also guaranteed, whereas the values of straight cereals vary dramatically from one batch to the next. Feeding cereals alone can also lead to deficiencies.

Just about the only problem with compound feeds is caused by owners who add unnecessary extras and in doing so destroy all the nutritionists' careful work. Adding half a scoop of oats in the mistaken idea that you are adding a bit of extra energy actually dilutes the feed and means that its perfect nutritional balance has been destroyed.

The extras you can add, and which are often beneficial, are some sort of chaff or short chop forage product, soaked sugar beet, salt and sliced apples and carrots. Adding short fibre bulks out the feed and makes the horse eat more slowly, which is much better for his digestive system and more akin to his natural way of feeding. Some products, such as Hi-Fi—made from alfalfa—are excellent hay replacers when good quality hay is hard to find.

Soaked sugar beet is a useful form of slow burn energy. Follow the manufacturer's instructions on soaking sugar beet pellets religiously; if they insufficiently soaked they can swell in the horse's stomach, leading to colic and other problems.

Vets and nutritionists now say that salt should be available to all horses and ponies. You can either put up a salt lick in the stable or on the field fence, or add a total of a tablespoonful of salt to the horse's daily feeds.

Apples and carrots are appreciated by most horses. Apples should be cut into quarters or smaller and carrots should be sliced lengthways to prevent the horse choking on them.

As compound feeds are formulated to meet your horse's nutritional requirements, you should not need to add extra supplements except under special circumstances. The main exception to this rule is if your horse or pony gets less than the minimum required amount to get his full nutritional quota—usually between two and three kg per day, which may be over the top in the case of some ponies and good doers. The way round this problem is to feed a broad spectrum vitamin and mineral supplement at half the manufacturer's recommended dosage.

Feed according to your horse's current workload, not what you would like him to be doing. Feeding a competition or event mix will not turn your horse into a high performance animal: unfortunately, the feed has not yet been developed that will make a horse jump higher or gallop faster!

If you find yourself being blinded by science, or have a particular problem, ring up your feed manufacturer. The best companies all employ nutritionists who will give free advice.

Starting work

If your horse is used to being ridden most days, your best plan is to get on him the day after he arrives. Do not be tempted to give him a week or two to settle in: he is a working animal. You bought him to ride, so enjoy it!

But do be sensible in your approach. If you are worried that he may be on edge, turn him out first and ride him in the afternoon or evening, depending on the time of year and the facilities available.

If for any reason he cannot be turned out, lunge him for ten minutes before you ride him. The idea is not to make him whiz round in circles so that he is worn out, but to get his brain into a working mode. Let him have a buck and a kick to start with, but then work on transitions between one pace and another so that he starts listening to you.

It is sensible to put protective boots on him to start with, even if you do not intend to use them all the time. If he does not wear a martingale, add a neckstrap; a spare stirrup leather buckled round his neck gives you extra security even if, as is likely, you do not need it.

You might want to ride in a schooling area for ten minutes before you go out, just to remind yourself what the horse feels like and to give him chance to get used to you. But do not expect to launch into a concentrated schooling session: that comes later.

Ask a friend with a reliable horse or pony to hack out with you. No horse is bombproof, and even the quietest ones have a wicked sense of humour at times, but try to enlist a sensible rider whose horse has a temperament to match. This is not going to be a fast hack, it is going to be a sedate and hopefully uneventful one!

Choose a quiet route that will last about an hour, allowing for the fact that you will be walking most of the time with the occasional trot when the going is good. Start off behind your escort, then move alongside when road conditions permit. When you feel confident, take the lead.

Your attitude is just as important as your riding ability. You need to be relaxed but positive: remember you bought this horse because you liked him and he gave you a nice ride, so expect to feel that way and you probably will. If you go out thinking that he is bound to spook and shy he undoubtedly will because your nervousness and tension will transmit itself to him.

If this is your first horse, or you are not used to riding different ones, you are likely be a little excited and/or apprehensive. Thinking positive is the best thing to do because you will give your horse confidence and the way he responds will boost your own sense of security.

Once you have ridden your horse two or three times you should both start to feel happier. Occasionally, a horse will settle in and then seem to test his rider out a little, perhaps because the rider is not as positive as the previous owner. This is when you have to be confident: think forwards all the time.

Some horses settle in a new home in a matter of days, whilst others take a bit longer. Once you feel he is starting to relax, book some lessons with a good, sympathetic instructor. This is the best way to establish a good relationship with your horse right from the start because a trainer with whom you have a good rapport will bring out the best in both of you.

If you have only ridden in a riding school, working your own horse can be bewildering at first. All of a sudden there is no one to say 'Go large' or 'Ride a 20-

metre circle at C' and so on. Your instructor will help you think for yourself and plan a varied and constructive work programme.

A good instructor will help you establish a partnership with your new horse.

The person who taught you at your riding school may be equally helpful now that you have your own horse, but unless they are used to assessing unknown quantities you may be better off finding a good freelance teacher. Find someone who specialises in the area or areas you hope to explore with your horse, whether it be show jumping, dressage, showing or whatever.

Someone who does successfully what you are aiming for but has no official qualifications may be better than a teacher with lots of letters after their name but little relevant practical experience. That is not meant to decry qualifications, just to point out that they are not always the be all and end all.

The other side of the coin is that just because someone is a good rider, it does not necessarily mean that they are a good teacher. Nothing is more dispiriting than an instinctive rider who cannot understand that you cannot always persuade your body to obey what your mind is telling it to do!

It is also important that your instructor likes your horse, or at least understands that you like him and want to make the most of him. An instructor can advise, but only you can decide whether or not you have found the right horse.

Try to budget for regular lessons, even if you can only manage once a fortnight or even once a month. Not only do they help you to set and work to your goals, they also mean that if or when you hit a problem, you know that help will soon be at hand.

Owning a horse or pony is never straightforward, even if you have the most expensive, well-schooled animal money can buy. There will always be lows as well as highs and there will always be times when you seem to take two steps back for every one step forwards.

But if you like a challenge—and you would not have taken on your horse unless you did—you will find that he adds a new dimension to your life. You may be a lot poorer, but you will never be bored!

Index